Internet Research

ILLUSTRATED Seventh Edition

Don I. Barker/Melissa S. Barker

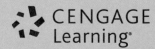
CENGAGE
Learning·

Australia · Brazil · Japan · Korea · Mexico · Singapore · Spain · United Kingdom · United States

CENGAGE
Learning·

Internet Research—Illustrated, Seventh Edition
Donald I. Barker, Melissa S. Barker

Senior Product Team Manager: Marjorie Hunt

Associate Product Manager: Amanda Lyons

Senior Content Developer: Christina Kling-Garrett

Marketing Manager: Gretchen Swann

Contributing Author: Kim Crowley

Development Editor: Kim Crowley

Senior Content Project Manager: GEX Publishing
  Services

Copyeditor: GEX Publishing Services

Proofreader: Lisa Weidenfeld

Indexer: Rich Carlson

QA Manuscript Reviewers: Serge Palladino,
  Jeff Schwartz

Cover Designer: GEX Publishing Services

Cover Artist: ©vector-RGB/Shutterstock

Composition: GEX Publishing Services

For product information and technology assistance, contact us at
Cengage Learning Customer & Sales Support, 1-800-354-9706

For permission to use material from this text or product, submit all
requests online at **www.cengage.com/permissions**
Further permissions questions can be emailed to
permissionrequest@cengage.com

Library of Congress Control Number: 2013950003
ISBN-13: 978-1-285-85412-0
ISBN-10: 1-285-85412-8

Cengage Learning
200 First Stamford Place, 4th Floor
Stamford, CT 06902
USA

Cengage Learning is a leading provider of customized learning solutions
with office locations around the globe, including Singapore, the United
Kingdom, Australia, Mexico, Brazil, and Japan. Locate your local office at:
www.cengage.com/global

Cengage Learning products are represented in Canada by
Nelson Education, Ltd.

For your course and learning solutions, visit **www.cengage.com**

Purchase any of our products at your local college store or at our
preferred online store **www.cengagebrain.com**

Trademarks:
Some of the product names and company names used in this book have
been used for identification purposes only and may be trademarks or
registered trademarks of their respective manufacturers and sellers.

Printed in the United States of America
1 2 3 4 5 6 7 19 18 17 16 15 14 13

Contents

Internet 2013

New! Learning Outcomes

Every 2-page lesson in this book now contains a green **Learning Outcomes box** that states the learning goals for that lesson.

- **What is a learning outcome?** A learning outcome states what a student is expected to know or be able to do after completing a lesson. Each learning outcome is skills-based or knowledge-based and is *measurable*. Learning outcomes map to learning activities and assessments.

- **How do students benefit from learning outcomes?** Learning outcomes tell students exactly what skills and knowledge they are *accountable* for learning in that lesson. This helps students study more efficiently and effectively and makes them more active learners.

- **How do instructors benefit from learning outcomes?** Learning outcomes provide clear, measurable, skills-based learning goals that map to various high-quality learning activities and assessments. A **Learning Outcomes Map**, available for each unit in this book, maps every learning outcome to the learning activities and assessments shown below.

Learning Outcomes Map to These Learning Activities:

1. **Book lessons:** Step-by-step tutorial on one skill presented in a two-page learning format

Learning Outcomes Map to These Assessments:

1. **End-of-Unit Exercises: Concepts Review** (screen identification, matching, multiple choice); **Skills Review** (hands-on review of each lesson); **Independent Challenges** (hands-on, case-based review of specific skills); **Visual Workshop** (activity that requires critical thinking skills).
2. **Exam View Test Banks:** Objective-based questions you can use for online or paper testing.

Learning Outcomes Map

A **Learning Outcomes Map**, contained in the Instructor Resources, provides a listing of learning activities and assessments for each learning outcome in the book.

Learning Outcomes Map
Intenet Research Illustrated 7th Edition
Unit A: Searching the Internet Effectively

KEY:
IC=Independent Challenge
VW=Visual Workshop

	Concepts Review	Skills Review	IC1	IC2	IC3	IC4	VW	Test Bank
Understand Internet Search Tools								
Identify search tools	✓	✓						✓
Create an Internet Research Strategy								
Develop a search strategy	✓	✓	✓	✓	✓		✓	✓
Evaluate results	✓	✓						✓
Refine a search	✓	✓						✓
Identify the Right Keywords								
Develop a topic sentence		✓	✓	✓		✓	✓	✓
Select keywords								
Find related terms		✓	✓	✓	✓		✓	✓
Perform a basic search								
Conduct a basic search	✓	✓		✓	✓		✓	✓
Compare search results		✓						
Add keywords								
Search with additional keywords	✓	✓			✓			✓
Use phrase searching								
Conduct a phrase search								✓

Preface

Welcome to *Internet Research - Illustrated, Seventh Edition*. This book has a unique design: Each skill is presented on two facing pages, with steps on the left and screens on the right. The layout makes it easy to learn a skill without having to read a lot of text and flip pages to see an illustration.

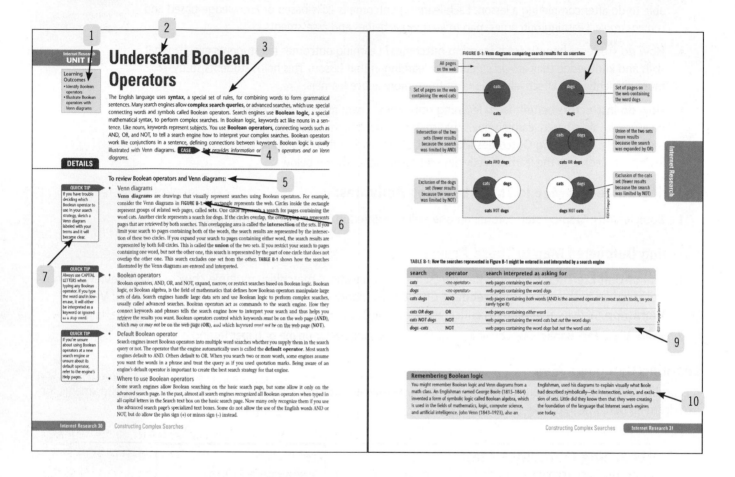

1. New! Learning Outcomes box lists measurable learning goals for which a student is accountable in that lesson.

2. Each two-page lesson focuses on a single skill.

3. Introduction briefly explains why the lesson skill is important.

4. A case scenario motivates the steps and puts learning in context.

5. Step-by-step instructions and brief explanations guide students through each hands-on lesson activity.

6. New! Figure references are now in red bold to help students refer back and forth between the steps and screenshots.

7. Tips and troubleshooting advice, right where you need it—next to the step itself.

8. New! Larger screenshots with green callouts now keep students on track as they complete steps.

9. Tables provide summaries of helpful information such as button references or keyboard shortcuts.

10. Clues to Use yellow boxes provide useful information related to the lesson skill.

Instructor Resources

This book is an ideal learning tool for a wide range of learners—the "rookies" will find the clean design easy to follow and focused with only essential information presented, and the "hotshots" will appreciate being able to move quickly through the lessons to find the information they need without reading a lot of text. The design also makes this a great reference after the course is over! See the illustration on the left to learn more about the pedagogical and design elements of a typical lesson.

About Edition

- **Coverage** — Helps students learn strategies for conducting effective searches on the Internet, including performing basic searches, and using Boolean search techniques and advanced search operators. Also covers specialty searches and subject directories, and includes a full chapter on social media searches. Helps students learn to evaluate Web pages for usefulness and authority.

- **New! Learning Outcomes** — Each lesson displays a green Learning Outcomes box that lists skills-based or knowledge-based learning goals for which students are accountable. Each Learning Outcome maps to a variety of assessments. (See the inside cover of this book for more information.)

- **New! Updated Design** — This edition features many new design improvements to engage students — including larger lesson screenshots with green callouts, and a refreshed Unit Opener page.

- **New! Independent Challenge 4: Explore** — This new case-based assessment activity allows students to explore new skills and use creativity to solve a problem or create a project.

Assignments

This book includes a wide variety of high quality assignments you can use for practice and assessment. Assignments include:

- **Concepts Review** — Multiple choice, matching, and screen identification questions.
- **Skills Review** — Step-by-step, hands-on review of every skill covered in the unit.
- **Independent Challenges 1–3** — Case projects requiring critical thinking and application of the unit skills. The Independent Challenges increase in difficulty. The first one in each unit provides the most hand-holding; the subsequent ones provide less guidance and require more critical thinking and independent problem solving.
- **Independent Challenge 4: Explore** — Case project that lets students explore new skills that are related to the core skills covered in the unit and is often more open ended, allowing students to use creativity to complete the assignment.
- **Visual Workshop** — Critical thinking exercises that require students to complete a task by looking at a completed solution; they must apply the skills they've learned in the unit and use critical thinking skills to complete a task.

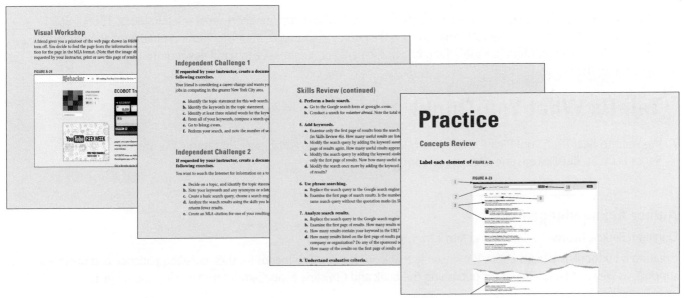

Instructor Resources

This book comes with a wide array of high-quality technology-based, teaching tools to help you teach and to help students learn. The following teaching tools are available for download at our Instructor Companion Site. Simply search for this text at *login.cengage.com*. An instructor login is required.

- **New! Learning Outcomes Map** — A detailed grid for each unit (in Excel format) shows the learning activities and assessments that map to each learning outcome in that unit.

- **Instructor's Manual** — Available as an electronic file, the Instructor's Manual includes lecture notes with teaching tips for each unit.

- **Sample Syllabus** — Prepare and customize your course easily using this sample course outline.

- **PowerPoint Presentations** — Each unit has a corresponding PowerPoint presentation covering the skills and topics in that unit that you can use in lectures, distribute to your students, or customize to suit your course.

- **Figure Files** — The figures in the text are provided on the Instructor Resources site to help you illustrate key topics or concepts. You can use these to create your own slide shows or learning tools.

- **Solutions Document** — This document outlines the solutions for the end-of-unit Concepts Review, Skills Review, Independent Challenges and Visual Workshops.

- **ExamView Test Banks** — ExamView is a powerful testing software package that allows you to create and administer printed, computer (LAN-based), and Internet exams. Our ExamView test banks include questions that correspond to the skills and concepts covered in this text, enabling students to generate detailed study guides that include page references for further review. The computer-based and Internet testing components allow students to take exams at their computers, and also save you time by grading each exam automatically.

Key Facts About Using This Book

Internet connection needed: To complete the exercises in this book your computer must be connected to the Internet.

System requirements: This book was written and tested using Windows 8. The browsers used for any steps that require a browser are Internet Explorer 10 and Firefox.

Screen resolution: This book was written and tested on computers with monitors set at a resolution of 1366×768. If your screen shows more or less information than the figures in this book, your monitor is probably set at a higher or lower resolution. If you don't see something on your screen, you might have to scroll down or up to see the object identified in the figure.

Tell Us What You Think!

We want to hear from you! Please email your questions, comments, and suggestions to the Illustrated Series team at: **illustratedseries@cengage.com**

Author Acknowledgements

Donald I. Barker, Melissa S. Barker, and Kim T.M. Crowley

Creating a textbook is a team effort. We sincerely thank our families and friends for their unfailing patience and generous support, as well as Marjorie Hunt for publishing the book and Christina Kling-Garrett for managing the project.

Searching the Internet Effectively

CASE ▶ You work in the city planning office in Portland, Oregon. The city is working toward becoming more energy independent, and you are to create a list of web resources on alternative energy. Although you use the web, you realize your skills need some polishing to do a quality job. You ask your friend, Bob Johnson, a reference librarian at a Portland University library, to help you learn the basics of Internet searching.

Unit Objectives

After completing this unit, you will be able to:

- Understand Internet search tools
- Create an Internet research strategy
- Identify the right keywords
- Perform a basic search
- Add keywords
- Use phrase searching
- Analyze search results
- Understand evaluative criteria
- Evaluate a web page
- Cite online resources

Files You Will Need

No files needed.

©vector-RGB/Shutterstock

Understand Internet Search Tools

The **World Wide Web** is an enormous repository of information stored on millions of computers all over the world. The **Internet** is a vast global network of interconnected smaller networks. You use the Internet to connect to information on the web. As the amount of information on the Internet grows exponentially, finding the reliable information you need can be a challenging task. A wide variety of **Internet search tools** are available that locate and catalogue the information on the web, making it easier and quicker to locate the information you need. Most of the search tools require you to compose and enter a **search query**, which tells a search tool specifically what information you want. Search tools can be divided into four major categories: search engines, metasearch engines, specialized search engines, and social media search engines. Different search tools are better suited for finding different types of information, and no single tool searches the entire Internet. **FIGURE A-1** illustrates the four types of search tools and the areas of the web they cover. **CASE** *Before you start your search for web pages about alternative energy, Bob gives you a brief overview of search tools.*

DETAILS

Types of search tools include the following:

- **Search engines** enable you to locate web pages that contain keywords you enter in a search form. **Keywords** are the nouns and verbs, and sometimes important adjectives, which describe the major concepts of your search topic. A program called a **spider** crawls or scans the web to index the keywords on web pages. When you enter keywords in a search engine, it uses these indexes or indices to find links to the most relevant web pages containing these keywords. Since this process requires an exact keyword match, it provides a narrow search of the web that works well for finding specific content. Another limiting factor is the kind of information that search engines can easily locate. As video and audio content have become a sizable part of the web, it has become more difficult for search engines to correctly index the entire web. To find out more about search engines, visit Search Engine Watch at searchenginewatch.com or Search Engine Showdown at searchengineshowdown.com.

- **Metasearch engines** offer a single search form to query multiple search engines simultaneously. As with search engines, you enter keywords to retrieve links to web pages that contain matching information. Search results are compiled from other search engines, rather than from the web. Metasearches are useful for quickly providing the highest-ranked results from multiple search engines. Better metasearch engines remove duplicate results and rank the results based on relevancy to your query. Unfortunately, these results might not be optimal; the best search engines are often excluded from a metasearch because they charge fees, which metasearch engine providers decline to pay.

QUICK TIP
Major search engines constantly work toward being able to search parts of the web that are currently invisible to their spiders.

- **Specialized search engines** allow you to find information that is "invisible" to traditional search engines because it is stored in proprietary databases, specialty directories, or reference sites. The vast majority of the information on the web is in this invisible area, usually called the **deep web**. To retrieve this information, you must go to a specific site and use its unique search interface. Although many of these sites can be searched with specialized search engines, others require a subscription or charge a fee for access. Many of these are available at libraries.

- **Social media search engines** enable you to locate content created by the masses and experts on a wide variety of social media platforms. **Social media platforms** include social networks, blogs, microblogs, video and photo sharing sites, social news sites, and Q&A (Question-and-Answer) sites. Finding relevant information on the growing number of social media platforms can be a challenge. Social media search engines have emerged as a powerful means to automatically search multiple social media sites simultaneously in real time.

FIGURE A-1: Internet search tools

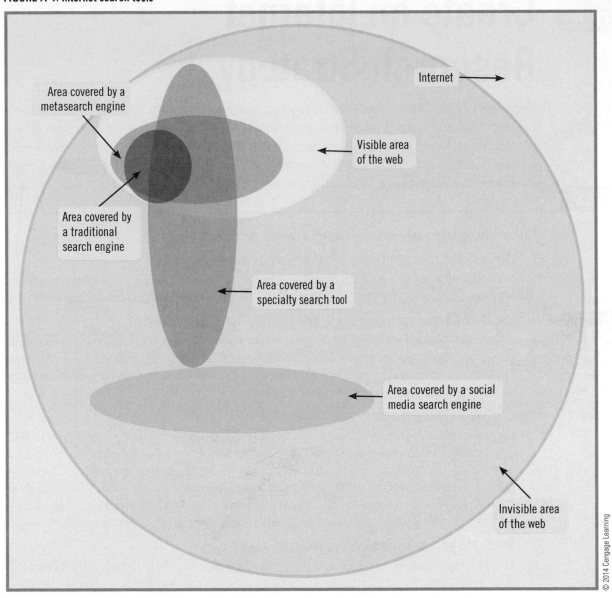

Area covered by a metasearch engine

Internet

Visible area of the web

Area covered by a traditional search engine

Area covered by a specialty search tool

Area covered by a social media search engine

Invisible area of the web

Using a search toolbar

Google, Microsoft, and Yahoo! provide search toolbars that enable you to search the Internet from your desktop or browser, without actually visiting the search engines. Each toolbar is closely tied to its parent search engine, and they share many features such as the ability to block pop-ups, automatically complete forms, and protect against spyware. The Google toolbar checks the spelling of your queries, translates English words into other languages, and blocks pop-ups. The Bing toolbar provides buttons that when you point to them, display the current page on various popular sites, such as Facebook, or get current weather or stock information. The Yahoo! toolbar provides one-click access to features on its site, such as Yahoo! Mail, weather, and news. (You download these search toolbars from their respective company web sites. Just search the sites using the toolbar name.)

Create an Internet Research Strategy

Learning Outcomes
• Develop a search strategy
• Evaluate results
• Refine a search

Before you begin a search on the Internet, you first need to focus on what information you want and how you might find it. If you start your online searching without giving thought to a plan or strategy, you can produce an overwhelming list of largely useless results. **FIGURE A-2** illustrates seven steps that significantly increase the likelihood of finding the information you need in a timely manner. **CASE** ▶ *Bob suggests you develop a research strategy, following the guidelines in* **FIGURE A-2**.

DETAILS

Follow these steps when formulating a research strategy:

• **Define your topic and note initial keywords**

Ask yourself what you want to end up with when you finish your research. Write down your topic. Note keywords and phrases. You don't have to use complete sentences, but be thorough in identifying concepts.

• **Locate background information and identify additional keywords**

If you initially know very little about the topic you are researching, look for general information in encyclopedias, periodicals, and reference sources first. They can give you a solid foundation for your research and provide keywords to use in your search. When you come across potentially useful keywords, note them and their correct spellings so you can use them in your search query.

• **Choose the proper search tool**

Use the search tools that are best suited to retrieving the type of information you want to find. **TABLE A-1** lists the most common search tools and provides information on how to select the best tool for your research needs. If you want specific content, search engines or metasearch engines are appropriate. When seeking information not normally tracked by these tools, turn to specialized search engines. When informed opinions or reviews and comments by the masses are useful, as in product evaluations, social media search engines are required. Combining these search tools provides the most thorough approach.

• **Translate your question into an effective search query**

The first step in translating a question into an effective search query is to identify the keywords that best describe the topic. You can also combine keywords with search operators and parentheses to construct complex searches for greater accuracy.

• **Perform your search**

Search engines offer a variety of different search forms that contain fields in which you enter information specific to your search. The information you provide produces **search results**.

• **Evaluate your search results**

The quantity and quality of results vary from one search engine to another. To ascertain the value of the information you find, you need to evaluate your search results by identifying who authored the web page or determining how current the information is.

• **Refine your search, if needed**

If the quality or quantity of results is not what you need, return to an earlier step in the process and use what you learned from your first pass through this process to refine your search. First, try fine-tuning your search query, and then try a different search tool. If you are still not satisfied with your results, you might need to reevaluate your keywords. Perhaps they are too specific or too general. If you are still unsuccessful in locating the required information, it is often helpful to return to the beginning and learn more about the topic so you identify more appropriate keywords.

FIGURE A-2: Developing a research strategy

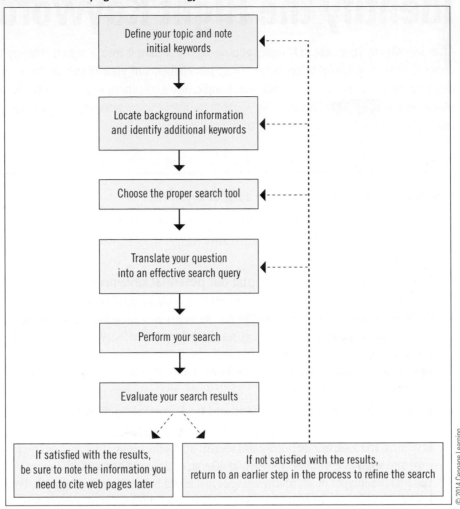

TABLE A-1: Common search tools

search tool	best for	where it searches	how to search	sample information	sample tools
Search engines	General or specific	Searches its own indexes that are compiled from data gathered from the web	Enter keywords, phrases, or complex search criteria	Alternative energy or solar panels	Google Yahoo! Bing
Metasearch engines	General or specific	Searches the indexes of multiple search engines simultaneously	Enter keywords, phrases, or complex search criteria	Alternative energy or solar panels	Dogpile Excite MetaCrawler
Specialized tools	More specific	Searches its own files or databases, directories, reference sites, government information, media, and search engines	Enter search term and browse directories	Latest news on solar panels	USA.gov SuperPages MagPortal
Social media search engines	More specific	Searches social media sites	Enter keywords, phrases, or complex search criteria, as well as browse directories	Opinions, reviews, and expert advice on solar panels	Social Mention Addict-o-matic Topsy

Identify the Right Keywords

Learning Outcomes
• Develop a topic sentence
• Select keywords
• Find related terms

After identifying your research topic, you need to translate it into a search strategy that optimizes your chances of finding useful information. The main elements in your search strategy are the keywords that describe the major concepts of your search topic. You enter these keywords into the search tool to return useful results. **CASE** ▶ *Bob provides you with the following guidelines to help you create a list of keywords to use in your search for web resources on alternative energy.*

DETAILS

Follow these guidelines to create a list of keywords:

- **Write a sentence or two that summarizes your research topic**

  You want to find web resources on alternative energy. The sentence shown in **FIGURE A-3** demonstrates how to state your research topic.

- **Study the research topic and pull out potential keywords**

  You look at this topic and decide the words that could be used as keywords are *alternative* and *energy*. You circle these words, as shown in **FIGURE A-4**. By identifying these words, you are starting to turn your topic statement into terms that an Internet search tool can use effectively. Remember, these are the words you expect to appear on the web pages that might be useful for your project. Search engines do not index words such as the articles *a, an,* and *the*. See **TABLE A-2** for typical words that do not qualify as keywords, also known as **stop words**.

- **If necessary, define the keywords and find general background information on your topic**

  If you know very little about the topic you are researching, some initial research can help you identify useful keywords. You look in a dictionary and see that *alternative energy* is energy from non-fossil fuels. It mentions solar and wind as examples. You then look in an encyclopedia to read a bit more about alternative energy. You find other types of alternative energies that might be useful, including water, biomass, and geothermal. **FIGURE A-5** illustrates how to list the keywords you identified for your research topic.

QUICK TIP
Keep this list of keywords and related keywords handy, as you might find new words if you need to refine your search later using different search tools.

- **Identify related terms using keyword generators**

  Keyword generators are tools that produce related keywords by using synonyms, plurals, misspellings, and other grammatical inflections. Web site designers use keyword generators to identify words that searchers will most likely use when trying to locate the content at a particular web site. However, keyword generators can also be quite useful for searchers looking for the best possible keywords to find a topic. In addition to identifying related words to search on, keyword generators such as the Google AdWords Keyword Tool (which you can find at adwords.google.com) reveal the number of monthly searches using different variations of keywords. This can be useful because it indicates the keywords other people are using to find content. By using a keyword generator to expand your list of keywords, you help ensure that your queries are broad enough to find web pages not indexed under the exact keywords in your initial list. **FIGURE A-6** shows a list of related keywords generated by Google AdWords Keyword Tool.

TABLE A-2: Common words that are not useful in most searches

parts of speech	examples
Articles	a, an, the
Conjunctions and prepositions	and, or, but, in, of, for, on, into, from, than, at, to
Adjectives and adverbs	as, also, probably, however, very
Pronouns and verbs	this, that, these, those, is, be, see, do

FIGURE A-3: Write down your research topic statement

I want to find web resources on alternative energy.

FIGURE A-4: Circle the keywords in your statement

I want to find web resources on (alternative) (energy).

FIGURE A-5: Identify and list additional keywords

Keywords

alternative

energy

solar

wind

water

biomass

geothermal

FIGURE A-6: Identify synonyms and related words

Keywords	Synonyms & Related Terms
alternative	renewable, sustainable
energy	power
solar	panels, photovoltaic
wind	turbines, windmills
water	hydropower, hydroelectric
biomass	waste-to-energy, bioenergy
geothermal	heat, pumps

Perform a Basic Search

Learning Outcomes
• Conduct a basic search
• Compare search results

Search engines often differ in how they perform a basic search. An effective search statement at one search engine might not produce the best results at another. You can overcome these inconsistencies by using a trial-and-error approach to searching. At each search engine, try subtle variations on the search, changing your wording slightly. Note which search engines perform best for different kinds of searches. **CASE** ➤ *You are ready to conduct a basic search using keywords you identified for alternative energy.*

STEPS

1. **Start your web browser, type** google.com **in the Address bar, then press** [Enter]
   The Google search form opens, as shown in **FIGURE A-7**.

2. **Click in the** Search text box, **then type** s
   A list of suggested keywords beginning with *s* appears below the Search text box. This feature is called Google Instant Search. Note that this list is localized, meaning that the suggested keywords vary depending upon where Google thinks you are located geographically. As you type each additional character of your keywords, the list of suggestions changes. In addition, Google Instant Search displays a guess as to the rest of the characters in the keywords in gray, and displays search results for that complete search phrase. You can press [Enter] to accept the guessed keywords in the Search text box, click one of the other suggested search terms in the list, or continue typing your keywords.

3. **Type** solar energy, **then click the** Search button
   Your results for solar energy should look similar to **FIGURE A-8**. The pages that best match the search query are listed at the top. However, sometimes the top results appear in a shaded background, with the label *Ads*. Many search engines, like Google, accept payment for higher placement, so these sites are listed at the top where you typically expect the best matching results.

4. **Delete your previous query in the** Search text box, **type** solar power, **then press** [Enter]
   Notice that the browser displays a different number of results for this search than the last. One small change in a search query can radically change the number and quality of search results. In addition, your results might include several web pages from the same web site, if each of those pages contains text that matches your search query. You decide to try your search using Bing.

5. **Click the** Back button **in your browser window**
   The search results for the first search you performed (for *solar energy*) again appear in the browser window.

6. **Open a new tab or browser window, type** bing.com **in the Address bar, then press** [Enter]
   The Bing search form opens.

7. **Click in the** Search text box, **type** solar energy, **then press** [Enter]
   Like Google, Bing lists suggested keywords below the Search text box as you type. Notice the number of results returned in Bing.

8. **Compare the number of results found for this search with the number of results found for the first search you performed in the first tab or browser window using Google**
   The number of results returned by each search engine differs significantly, even though the search query was the same.

9. **In the tab or window containing the Google search results, click the** Forward button
   The results of your second search (for *solar power*) again appear in the window.

10. **In the tab or window containing the Bing search results, delete your previous query in the** Search text box, **type** solar power, **then press** [Enter]
    Notice again that the number of results for this search differs both from the previous search conducted in Bing and from the number of results found for this search query in Google.

FIGURE A-7: Google search form

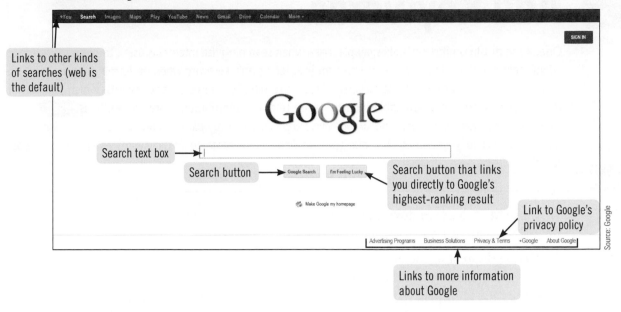

FIGURE A-8: Google search results

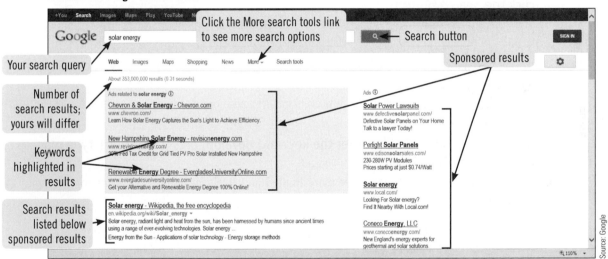

Why do search results vary with different search engines?

Search engines use different criteria for ranking and ordering search results. Typically, search engines factor in the location of the keywords on the web pages returned in search results, and list those web pages in which the keywords appear in the page titles or at the top of pages first. Frequency of keywords (the number of times keywords appear in a web page) is another factor search engines use to determine the relevancy of a web page. While location and frequency play a key role in how most search engines rank search results, search engines also account for other criteria, such as the number of external pages from quality sites pointing to a web page. So when your results are ranked for relevancy, different search engines will likely list results in a different order. Moreover, some search engines crawl and index more pages than others and do so more often. Hence, search engines usually differ in the number of results of they produce.

Add Keywords

One of the most common mistakes people make when searching the Internet is using too few keywords to adequately describe a topic. In fact, some people enter a single keyword when performing a search, which typically returns thousands, if not millions, of search results. Entering several keywords, which narrows or focuses your search results, enables you to locate relevant information more efficiently. **CASE** *You want to locate more specific information on developing a solar energy plan for Portland, so you decide to add some keywords to your search. You also want to find out whether adding keywords really improves your search results.*

STEPS

1. **Close the tab or window containing the Bing search results**
   The tab containing the Google search results is the active tab.

2. **Delete the text in the Search text box**
   You decide to start with the basic search terms you used previously.

3. **Type solar energy in the Search text box, then click the Search button**
   On the page listing the search results, a count of the total results appears at the top of the search results page. Because the number of results is quite large and the page descriptions are not particularly relevant to using solar energy as an alternative power source for a city, you decide to add the keyword *city* to your query.

4. **In the Search text box, click after the keyword energy, press [Spacebar], type city, then click the Search button**
   This search returns far fewer results, as illustrated in **FIGURE A-9**. In addition, the page descriptions indicate that the information is more closely related to solar energy use in a city.

5. **In the Search text box, click after the keyword city, press [Spacebar], type develop, then click the Search button**
   Notice that the number of results is now even smaller and more closely related to how to develop solar energy for a city.

6. **In the Search text box, click after the keyword develop, press [Spacebar], type plan, then click the Search button**
   Your number of results is now even more limited and likely to be more relevant for your project. See **FIGURE A-10**.

FIGURE A-9: Search results narrowed by adding a keyword

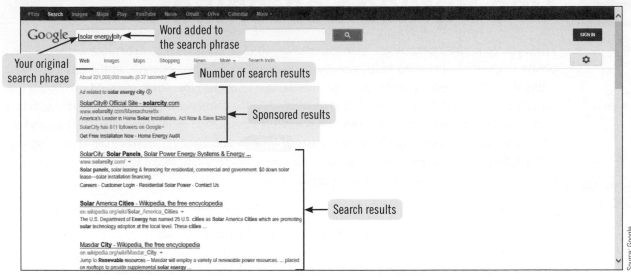

FIGURE A-10: Search results narrowed further

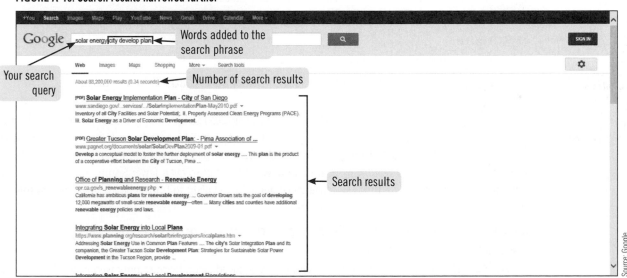

Arranging keywords

The order in which you place keywords in a search can be very important. Placing your most important keywords at the beginning of your search query causes a search engine to display results featuring the more important keywords at the top of your search results. For example, the keywords *hybrid electric vehicle* cause a search engine to first look for web pages containing the word *hybrid*, then *electric*, and finally, *vehicle*. Reversing the order of this search query (that is, *vehicle electric hybrid*) puts less emphasis on the keywords *hybrid* and *electric*, hence impacting the sequence of your search results. Depending on how the search engine finds results pages, it might also change the number of your search results.

Use Phrase Searching

When you construct a search with more than one keyword, you often need two or more words to be in a phrase rather than appearing independently on the results pages. For example, in the previous lesson, some of the results pages found were pages that happen to contain the words *solar* and *energy*, but they weren't actually about solar energy. To find these words in the correct order, you need to phrase search. In many search tools, **phrase searching** is accomplished by putting quotation marks (" ") around the words you want to appear together in your results. **CASE** ▶ *Bob suggests that your multi-keyword searches can be refined even more with phrase searching. You want to have the most meaningful results returned, so you decide to try some phrase searches and compare the results.*

STEPS

1. **Type bing.com in your browser's Address bar, then press [Enter]**

   The search form for Bing opens. A list of trending searches on Bing (labeled POPULAR NOW) appears below the Search text box. **Trending searches** are current popular searches by others that use the keywords you typed or similar terms. If you conducted a search on Bing previously during your current session on the computer, the search terms you used appear to the right of the trending searches under the heading "SEARCH HISTORY."

2. **Click in the Search text box, type bioenergy center, then click the Search button**

   FIGURE A-11 illustrates the results for the search using these two keywords. A count of the total results appears just below the Search text box, and is followed by a list of results.

3. **Delete the text in the Search text box, type center bioenergy, then click the Search button**

   This search returns fewer results than the first one.

QUICK TIP
Even though the phrase search returns far fewer results than the searches using two words, your first results might be the same, depending on how the search tool finds results pages.

4. **Click in the Search text box, edit the search query so it reads "bioenergy center", then click the Search button**

   Be sure to type quotation marks around the words *bioenergy center* to tell Bing to search for an exact phrase. You should now have fewer results than in the first two searches. This search has located only web pages that contain the exact phrase *bioenergy center*. **FIGURE A-12** compares the two-word searches with the phrase search. If you add another word to your search phrase, it will return even fewer results. You know the U.S. Department of Energy (DOE) funds a bioenergy center, and you want to find web pages that discuss this, so you decide to include this in your search phrase.

5. **Click in the Search text box, edit the search query so it reads "doe bioenergy center", then click the Search button**

   See **FIGURE A-13**. The number of results is significantly reduced again because only web pages that contain the phrase *DOE bioenergy center* are returned.

FIGURE A-11: Two-keyword search results in Bing

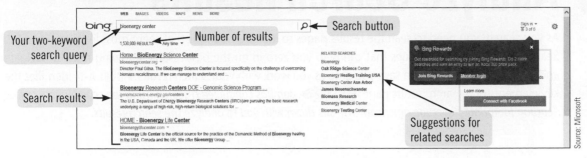

Your two-keyword search query

Number of results

Search button

Search results

Suggestions for related searches

Source: Microsoft

FIGURE A-12: Comparing two-word searches with a phrase search

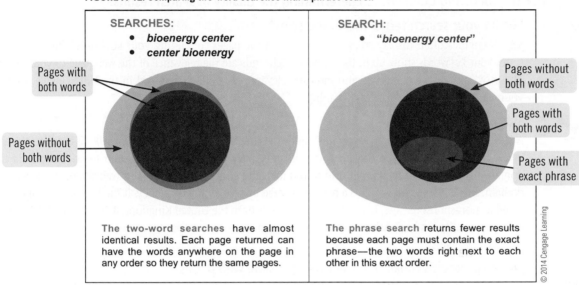

SEARCHES:
- *bioenergy center*
- *center bioenergy*

SEARCH:
- *"bioenergy center"*

Pages with both words

Pages without both words

Pages without both words

Pages with both words

Pages with exact phrase

The two-word searches have almost identical results. Each page returned can have the words anywhere on the page in any order so they return the same pages.

The phrase search returns fewer results because each page must contain the exact phrase—the two words right next to each other in this exact order.

© 2014 Cengage Learning

FIGURE A-13: Phrase search results in Bing

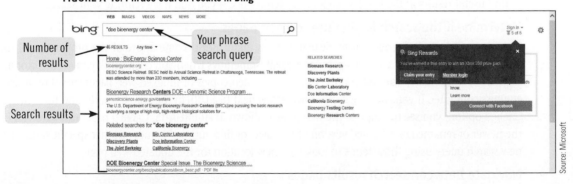

Number of results

Your phrase search query

Search results

Source: Microsoft

Other ways to search using phrases

Most search engines allow phrase searching but not all in the same way. Most use quotation marks around words to indicate a phrase. However, some might automatically assume you are looking for a phrase when you enter two words in the Search text box, in which case quotation marks are redundant, but harmless. Some search engines might provide a drop-down menu or check box with an option for "exact phrase." Others might include an additional Search text box labeled "with this exact phrase." Sometimes the option for a phrase search might appear on an advanced search page. Use the Help or Search Tip pages at each search engine to learn how it uses and interprets phrase searching.

Analyze Search Results

As you search, you need to scan the results pages to identify web sites that seem most likely to be useful. Search results pages offer clues that can help you zero in on the best results. Knowing how to navigate and read the results page can save you time as you work with your search results. **FIGURE A-14** identifies the key elements of a search results page. **CASE** *Bob has conducted a search using the search query reduce "carbon footprint" "average american". He sits down with you to analyze the search results.*

DETAILS

Use the following guidelines in determining the quality of search results:

• **Locate your search terms within the search result**

Search engines often display snippets of text from the pages containing your keywords. The number of times your keywords show up in the snippet might indicate the relevance of the web page to your search. The proximity of the words can also indicate relevance, as would a keyword in the URL. Google displays your search terms in bold for easy scanning.

• **Decipher the URL**

A URL is often **mnemonic**; that is, it indicates what the web site is about so that its URL is easier to remember. If the URL contains one of your keywords, it is likely to be mainly about your topic. The end of the domain name (.com, .edu, .jp, .uk, and so on) indicates either a certain type of web site or its geographic domain. If a URL ends in .gov, it is a page sponsored by a government agency. If the URL ends in .edu, it is an education-sponsored site. If a URL ends in .uk, it is from the United Kingdom. Being aware of this as you scan your results can be very helpful. A search for domain names or country domains results in lists you can check URLs against.

• **Note the result's ranking in the list of possible web pages**

Search engines use **algorithms**, or mathematical formulas, to rank each web site according to the terms used in your search query. Every search engine has a slightly different algorithm for figuring out which is the "best" web site, but all place their best picks at the top of the list. Generally speaking, you should be able to find useful results in the first few pages of search results. If you don't, try refining your search.

• **Determine if the search engine uses cached pages**

Sometimes links to web pages break. Search engines might not become aware of the problem until their spiders search that part of the web again. As a result, sometimes when you click a link you get an error message. Google has many **cached pages**, which are hidden copies of indexed web pages stored on a search engine's computer. If you click the green down arrow next to a URL in the search results, and then click the Cached option, you see the copy of the web page as shown in **FIGURE A-15**. Cached pages can help you find the newer or renamed or relocated version of the page, or find authors' names or other specific terms. Try a new search query using those terms to look for a new location for the updated web page.

• **Navigate between search results pages**

Search results are usually displayed about 10 to a page. Some searches return hundreds of pages. At Google, you navigate to a different page of results using the links located at the bottom of each results page, as shown in **FIGURE A-16**. Google, as well as some other engines, also offers search-refining options at the bottom of the page of results. Remember that the better your search strategy, the fewer pages of results you will need to examine to find relevant pages.

FIGURE A-14: Top of Google search results page

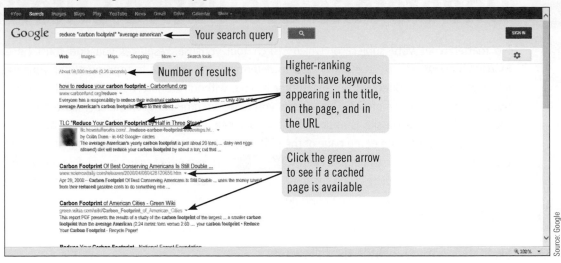

Your search query

Number of results

Higher-ranking results have keywords appearing in the title, on the page, and in the URL

Click the green arrow to see if a cached page is available

Source: Google

FIGURE A-15: Google's cache of a page from Carbonfund.org

Google's notification that this is a cached page

URL for and link to actual page

Date this image of the page was made

Google's image of the web page taken previously and cached

Source: Google

FIGURE A-16: Bottom of a Google search results page

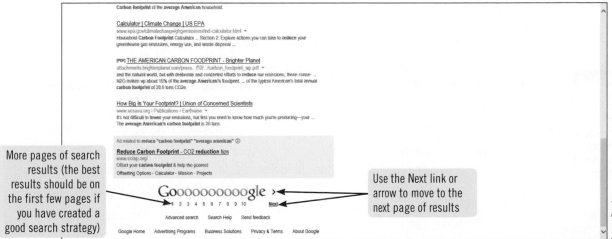

More pages of search results (the best results should be on the first few pages if you have created a good search strategy)

Use the Next link or arrow to move to the next page of results

Source: Google

Searching the Internet Effectively

Understand Evaluative Criteria

No matter what your subject or which search tool you use, resources you find must be evaluated. **Evaluative criteria** are standards used to determine if a web site is appropriate for your needs. Web information can go directly from the author to you, without the intervening editorial or review process used for most printed material. This requires you to be discriminating. **FIGURE A-17** illustrates the criteria to use in determining if a site is appropriate for your needs. **FIGURE A-18** shows an example of identifying evaluative criteria on the home page of the EESI web site, a non-profit organization that promotes policies that support clean and sustainable energy. **CASE** ▶ *In your recent searches, you found so many sites that you are concerned about selecting the most appropriate ones. You decide to review the criteria to use when evaluating web pages to determine which pages are appropriate.*

DETAILS

Evaluative criteria include the following:

- **Authority and accountability**

  Knowing the author's or owner's identity is key to determining how reliable the site is. This is usually the most important criterion to apply. Consider these questions:

  - Is the author or owner clearly identified? Are qualifications and associations identified?
  - Is there contact information for the author or owner? Is there an About Us link?
  - Is there an association with a university, a government agency, or an organization? If so, are there links?
  - Has the author written in the field? Does the owner specialize in the field? What kind of results do you get from a search on the author or owner?
  - Is there a bibliography? Are resources well documented?

- **Objectivity and accuracy**

  A site's objectivity and accuracy greatly affect its appropriateness. Consider these questions:

  - Does the author state the purpose of the site? Is the content presented as fact or as opinion? Does the author show any bias?
  - Is the publisher, sponsor, or host for the site identified?

- **Organization and design**

  Great content on a page can be defeated by poor design and functionality. Attractiveness and graphic features can mask a lack of meaningful content. Consider these questions:

  - Is the site well designed and functional? Is there a site map and Help page?
  - Is it easy to navigate? Do navigational buttons and internal links work?
  - Is it searchable? Are there a variety of ways to access material?

- **Scope**

  The scope of a site is the range of topics it covers. Consider these questions:

  - Is there introductory or summary information describing the scope of the site?
  - Who is the intended audience? Is the information presented appropriately for that audience?

- **Currency**

  Currency or timeliness might or might not be an issue for your search. Consider these questions:

  - Is there a creation or revision date?
  - Are there many broken links? (This might indicate the site is not being maintained.)

FIGURE A-17: Evaluative criteria contributing to a site's appropriateness

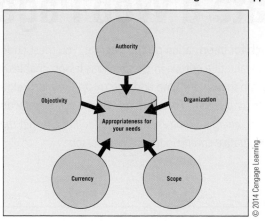

© 2014 Cengage Learning

FIGURE A-18: Identifying evaluative criteria on the EESI home page

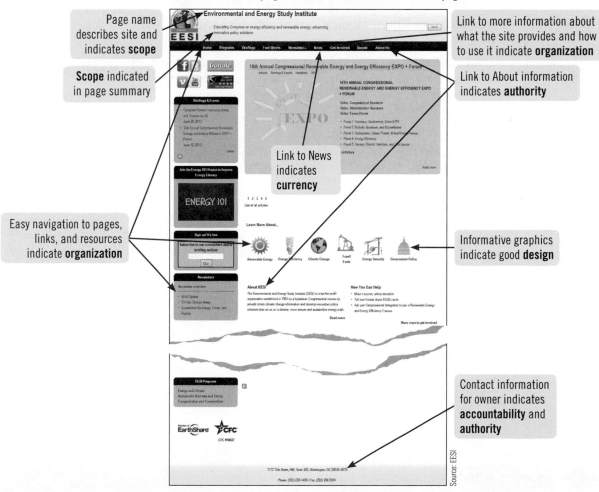

Page name describes site and indicates **scope**

Scope indicated in page summary

Link to more information about what the site provides and how to use it indicate **organization**

Link to About information indicates **authority**

Link to News indicates **currency**

Easy navigation to pages, links, and resources indicate **organization**

Informative graphics indicate good **design**

Contact information for owner indicates **accountability** and **authority**

Source: EESI

Understanding Wikipedia

Wikipedia.org is the largest, most popular, collaboratively built, free online encyclopedia. Since anyone can edit the information in Wikipedia, a common misconception is that Wikipedia is unreliable. In reality, comparative studies have shown that Wikipedia is actually as reliable as traditional encyclopedias. This is because when someone does accidently (or purposely) post erroneous information in Wikipedia, experts in the field typically identify and rectify the problem quickly. Although academics have been slow to accept Wikipedia as a valid source for citations, the number of scientific journals citing Wikipedia has grown significantly in recent years. As with any source, it is important to cross-check Wikipedia's information with other authoritative sources. Most Wikipedia topics provide a list of references you can use as a starting point.

Evaluate a Web Page

Learning Outcomes
- Determine a page's author
- Assess a web page's currency
- Evaluate a web page's organization and scope

Every time you search for information on the Internet, you must choose which web sites to include in your research. Using the evaluative criteria in the previous lesson enables you to quickly eliminate the least useful sites so that you can focus your time and energy on the most relevant ones. **CASE** ▶ *Bob the librarian mentions the web site for the Earth Policy Institute as one you might want to visit. It presents one organization's plan for how renewable energy resources can be used to help sustain the planet. You decide to visit the site and review it using the evaluative criteria in the previous lesson.*

STEPS

1. **Type earth-policy.org in your browser's Address bar, then press [Enter]**

   FIGURE A-19 illustrates the Earth Policy Institute's home page. You want to evaluate this site.

2. **Scan the page looking for indications of authority and objectivity**

   At the bottom of the page, the contact information provides a physical address, a telephone number, and an email address. The About EPI link leads to a page that describes the mission, goals, and activities of the organization, and includes links to testimonials, and a listing and description of the staff, and the members of the editorial board. You decide the authority, accountability, and objectivity of this site seem excellent.

3. **Scan the page looking for indications of scope**

   There is a summary of the site's purpose on the home page. The scope is indicated from the home page links to pages summarizing the mission and activities of the organization. The scope is also addressed on the About EPI page.

4. **Scan the page looking for indications of organization and currency**

   The design is attractive and functional. The menu bar at the top of the page provides clear navigation links for the site. The latest online postings show recent dates. The site map is organized and easy to use. All of the links work, there are several ways to find information, and the site is searchable. You decide this site is very well organized and current.

5. **Close all open browser tabs and windows**

Considering what others say about web pages

Another way to evaluate a web page is to consider how others value it. One way to determine this is to find out how many web pages link to the page you are evaluating. If a large number of quality sites link to a page, odds are that it contains authoritative and reputable information. To reveal the sites that link to a web page, you can use the Google link: advanced search operator; in the Google search form, type link: followed by the URL you want to check (for example, link:www.earth-policy.org). In the results page, Google will display a list of sites that link to the page you specified. You can examine the results to determine the number and quality of sites linking to the page. Another way to determine what others think about a web page is to visit Alexa.com. Type the URL of the page you want to check in the Search text box, and then click the Search button. At the top of the page that appears, click Get Details to the right of the URL you typed. The page that appears displays statistics about the web site, including what pages link to the site. You can examine the list to determine the number and quality of sites linking to the page.

FIGURE A-19: Earth Policy Institute home page

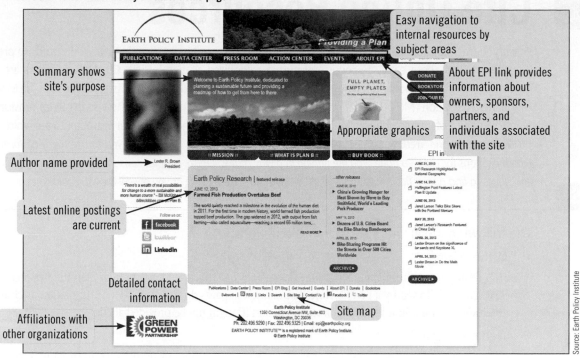

Summary shows site's purpose

Easy navigation to internal resources by subject areas

About EPI link provides information about owners, sponsors, partners, and individuals associated with the site

Appropriate graphics

Author name provided

Latest online postings are current

Detailed contact information

Site map

Affiliations with other organizations

Evaluating bias

No web page is totally objective. Commercial sites (.com or. biz) usually exist to sell something. Nonprofit organizations (.org) have opinions about their causes. Even an educational page (.edu) can be affected by its creator's views. Ideally, these sites divulge their positions openly, but sometimes this is not true.

Educational (.edu) and government (.gov) sites generally are more objective, or at least support their ideas with documented facts. As long as you can ascertain a page's bias, you can come to your own conclusions about its content.

Cite Online Resources

When you use information from web pages for classwork, you need to list them in your works cited. To present the relevant data about each site consistently, use a recognized citation format. **Citation formats** are style guides that standardize how citations are written. Two widely accepted citation formats are those of the Modern Language Association (MLA) and the American Psychological Association (APA). These style guides provide formats for all kinds of Internet information. For academic work, always check with your instructor to see which style guide format is preferred. See **TABLE A-3** for citation tips. **CASE** *Bob advises you to use the MLA format to record citations for the web pages you are finding in a way that will make your list consistent and easy for you or your colleagues to find again. Refer to* **FIGURE A-20**, **FIGURE A-21**, *and* **FIGURE A-22** *as you review the MLA guidelines.*

DETAILS

The following are elements used in MLA citations:

- **Author name**

  MLA format for author names is surname (last name) first, followed by a comma, then the personal name (first name), followed by a period. Note that many web pages do not display this information as clearly as the example. You might have to look to find it, and it might not be provided at all.

- **Web page title**

  MLA format requires the web page title, which is referred to as the title of the work, to be set in italics if it is independent, and within quotation marks if it is part of a larger work, with a period at the end of the title.

- **Web site title**

  MLA format requires the web site title to be italicized and followed by a period.

- **Web site publisher or sponsor**

  MLA format requires the web site publisher or sponsor to be listed next, followed by a comma. If no publisher or sponsor is listed, use *N.p.*

- **Date the web page was created or updated**

  MLA format for dates is *DD Month (Abbreviation) YYYY* followed by a period; for example, 15 Oct. 2016. Note that the months with only three or four letters in their names (May, June, and July) are not abbreviated. If there is no creation or update date, use *n.d.*

- **Date you viewed the web page**

  It is important to record the date you view a web page because pages change frequently. Use the same format as for the date the web page was created.

- **URL of the web page**

  The MLA does not require the inclusion of the URL (Internet address) of the web page because web addresses often change and a web page may appear in multiple places. If you chose to include the page's URL for easy reference (or if your instructors require it), it needs to be enclosed in angle brackets < >. If you need to break the URL into more than one line, break the line after a slash. Include a period after the right angle bracket.

Copyright and plagiarism

With the exception of works in the public domain, everything on the Internet is copyrighted, whether it is a web page, an image, or an audio file. (Note: Google's usage rights box, located on its Advanced Search page, includes options that let you filter search results to show only those that are "free to use or share" or "free to use or share, even commercially.") If you want to profit from someone else's copyrighted work, you must get permission from the author or creator. Copyright law is very complex, so consult a lawyer who specializes in copyright law. If you want to use part of someone else's work in a school assignment or paper, you generally can do so under the Fair Use exemption to copyright law. "Fair use" allows students and researchers to copy or use parts of other people's work for educational purposes. Always give credit by citing the source of the material you are using. If you don't credit an author or source, you are guilty of plagiarism.

FIGURE A-20: MLA citation style format for a web page

Element and Format	Example
Author Last Name, Author First Name.	Boswell, Wendy.
Web page title. or "web page title."	*DIY Alternative Energy Projects.*
Web site title	*Lifehacker.*
Web site publisher or sponsor,	Gawker Media,
Date page created or revised.	30 June 2006.
Date you viewed the web page.	25 June 2013.
<Full URL if required>.	<http://lifehacker.com/184452/diy-alternative-energy-projects>.

© 2014 Cengage Learning

FIGURE A-21: Citation in the MLA style for the web page below in Figure A-22

Boswell, Wendy. *DIY Alternative Energy Projects. Lifehacker.* Gawker Media, 30 June 2006. 25 June 2013. <http://lifehacker.com/184452/diy-alternative-energy-projects>.

© 2014 Cengage Learning

FIGURE A-22: Lifehacker page cited above in Figure A-21

© 2014 Cengage Learning
Source: Lifehacker

TABLE A-3: Citation tips

citation section	tips
Author	• When authors aren't named, skip this section. • If a corporate author is named, such as an association, institution, or government agency, use it in the author section.
Page title	• Sometimes the title is not clear; it might be under a banner or logo at the top of the page. • If you are citing the whole web site, you can skip this section, which is for a specific page.
URL	• The URL should not be underlined. • Some word processors automatically underline URLs, so you might need to remove the underline.
Date created/revised	• Sometimes a date can be difficult to find; it might be at the very bottom of the page. • When dates aren't provided, skip this section.
Date viewed	• If you print the page, the date is at the lower-right corner of your printout. • If you are not printing, note the date for your citation.

© 2014 Cengage Learning

Practice

Concepts Review

Label each element of FIGURE A-23.

FIGURE A-23

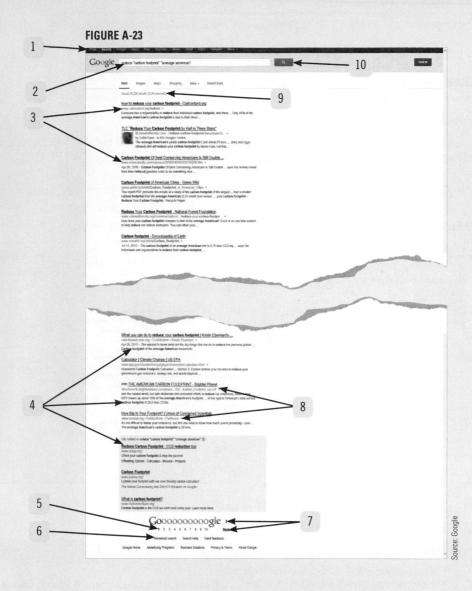

Source: Google

Match each term with the statement that best describes it.

11. **Deep web**

12. **Cached page**

13. **Search engine**

14. **Spider**

15. **Keywords**

16. **Result's ranking**

17. **Sponsored results**

a. A copy of a web page stored by a search engine

b. A web site that locates information on the Internet by searching web pages

c. Words that describe your search topic

d. Program that scans the web to index the keywords in web pages

e. Web pages that have paid for higher placement on search result pages

f. Web pages stored in proprietary databases, specialty directories, or reference sites

g. The order in which a search tool returns results, usually based on relevancy

Select the best answer from the list of choices.

18. Which of the following do you need to apply in order to ascertain the value of information you find?
   a. Specialty search tools
   b. Evaluative criteria
   c. Search forms
   d. Stop words

19. Phrase searching helps you find _____.
   a. wildcards
   b. synonyms
   c. words in the order you specify
   d. keywords

20. Which term describes current popular searches?
   a. Trending searches
   b. Phrase searches
   c. Keyword searches
   d. Algorithmic searches

21. In an MLA citation for a web page, if you include the URL, what symbols should enclose it?
   a. { }
   b. [ ]
   c. ( )
   d. < >

Skills Review

If requested by your instructor, create a document listing the answers to the questions asked in the following exercises.

1. **Understand Internet search tools.**
   a. Define *search query*.
   b. Describe search engines and how they work.
   c. Explain how a metasearch engine works.
   d. Describe how you find information on the deep web.
   e. Explain how using a social media search engine is different from using a metasearch engine.

2. **Create an Internet research strategy.**
   a. Describe the seven steps of an effective Internet research strategy, in order.
   b. Explain the importance of translating your topic into a search query and the value of refining your query to retrieve better results.

3. **Identify the right keywords.**
   a. Identify the two keywords in the following search topic: *I want to find information about volunteering abroad.*
   b. Think of at least three synonyms or related words for the keywords (they might all be for the same keyword).
   c. Explain what stop words are.

Skills Review (continued)

4. **Perform a basic search.**
   a. Go to the Google search form at **google.com**.
   b. Conduct a search for *volunteer abroad*. Note the total number of results returned.

5. **Add keywords.**
   a. Examine only the first page of results from the search you conducted using the search query *volunteer abroad* (in Skills Review 4b). How many useful results are listed?
   b. Modify the search query by adding the keyword *summer*, and then conduct the new search. Examine only the first page of results again. How many useful results appear now?
   c. Modify the search query by adding the keyword *student*, and then conduct the new search. Once again, examine only the first page of results. Now how many useful results appear?
   d. Modify the search once more by adding the keyword *college*. How many useful results appear on the first page of results?

6. **Use phrase searching.**
   a. Replace the search query in the Google search engine with *"volunteer abroad"*, and then conduct the new search.
   b. Examine the first page of search results. Is the number of results different from the search you conducted using the same search query without the quotation marks (in Skills Review 4b)?

7. **Analyze search results.**
   a. Replace the search query in the Google search engine with *volunteer*, and then conduct the search.
   b. Examine the first page of results. How many results were returned?
   c. How many results contain your keyword in the URL?
   d. How many results listed on the first page of results paid to be listed there? Is each sponsored result from a different company or organization? Do any of the sponsored results also appear in the list of results that are not sponsored?
   e. How many of the results on the first page of results are available as cached results from Google?

8. **Understand evaluative criteria.**
   a. Define *evaluative criteria*.
   b. According to the text, what are the five things to consider when evaluating a web page?
   c. What is one way you can determine the credibility of an author of a web page?

9. **Evaluate a web page.**
   a. Go to **idealist.org**.
   b. Evaluate this web page for authority and accountability. What areas of the page did you use to do this?
   c. Is this web page objective and accurate? Does it show any bias? How did you determine this?
   d. Describe the organization of the web site. Is it well organized in your opinion?
   e. Describe the scope of this web site. How did you determine this?
   f. Is the web page current? How do you know?

10. **Cite online resources.**
    a. Select one of the web pages returned by one of your searches.
    b. How would you write the citation for this web page using MLA format?

Independent Challenge 1

If requested by your instructor, create a document listing the answers to the questions asked in the following exercises.

Your friend is considering a career change and wants you to help with a web search. He wants to find information about jobs in computing in the greater New York City area.

   a. Identify the topic statement for this web search.
   b. Identify the keywords in the topic statement.
   c. Identify at least three related words for the keywords.
   d. From all of your keywords, compose a search query. Include at least one search phrase in the query.
   e. Go to **bing.com**.
   f. Perform your search, and note the number of search results returned.

Independent Challenge 2

If requested by your instructor, create a document listing the answers to the questions asked in the following exercises.

You want to search the Internet for information on a topic of your choosing.

   a. Decide on a topic, and identify the topic statement.
   b. Note your keywords and any synonyms or related terms.
   c. Create a basic search query, choose a search engine, and perform a search.
   d. Analyze the search results using the skills you learned in this unit, and then refine your search query so that it returns fewer results.
   e. Create an MLA citation for one of your resulting pages.

Independent Challenge 3

If requested by your instructor, create a document listing the answers to the questions asked in the following exercises.

In today's job market, many people find that technical skills, while necessary, are not sufficient for career advancement. Employability skills are equally important to maintaining a job and improving one's position. You decide to research how to improve your employability skills.

a. Go to **google.com**.

b. Conduct a search using the keyword *employability*. Examine the results on the first few pages.

c. Refine your search query to *employability skills*, and then search again. Examine the search results. Do you see many results that might give you information on improving your employability skills?

d. Modify your search query again to *improving employability skills*, and then repeat the search. Are the results more targeted to improving employability skills?

e. Modify your search query so it is a search phrase: *"improving employability skills"*. Conduct the search and examine the results. Do any of the results mention *soft skills*, *interpersonal skills*, or *emotional IQ*?

f. Choose one of the phrases mentioned in exercise e, add it to your search query, and then conduct the search. Did this yield more relevant results?

g. Delete your search query, and then conduct a new search using two of the phrases mentioned in exercise e. Does this search give you the same list of results, or are they different?

h. Finally, after reviewing the results you received in the searches you conducted in this Independent Challenge, create a new search query that contains search phrases and keywords that produce results that will help you advance in your field. For example, if you are in marketing, you could add *"marketing manager"* to your search query. Conduct the search and examine the results.

Independent Challenge 4: Explore

If requested by your instructor, create a document listing the answers to the questions asked in the following exercises.

You want to find information about the music of South Africa. You decide to use phrase searching to narrow your search results.

a. Go to **google.com**, and then conduct a search for *South Africa music*. Note the number of results.

b. Conduct a search for *zulu music*.

c. Conduct a search for *crossover music*. Note the number of results.

d. Conduct a phrase search for *"South Africa" zulu "crossover music"*. Note the number of results.

e. Which search yielded the fewest results? Why?

f. In a new browser window or tab, conduct the same search for *"South Africa" zulu "crossover music"* on **bing.com**. Compare the number of results to the number found when you conducted this search on Google. Why does the number of results differ?

g. In the tab or window containing the Google results, scroll to the bottom of the results page, click the Advanced search link, and then use the option to restrict the search to web sites in the region of South Africa. Note the number of results.

h. In the tab or window containing the Google results, use the Advanced Search page to add a restriction to the domain .za. Note the number of results. Also, examine the revised search phrase in the Search text box, and note the search operator and keyword that was added.

i. In the tab or window containing the Bing results, click in the Search text box, and then click the Advanced search link that appears below the Search text box. Use the option to restrict the search to web sites to the Country/Region of South Africa. Note the number of results. Also, examine the revised search phrase in the Search text box, and note the search operator and keyword that was added.

j. In the tab or window containing the Bing results, use the Advanced Search page to add a restriction to the domain .za. Note the number of results. Also, examine the revised search phrase in the Search text box, and note the search operator and keyword that was added.

k. In the tab or window containing the Bing results, delete the search operator and keyword from the Search text box that restricted the search to the region of South Africa. Note the number of results.

Visual Workshop

A friend gives you a printout of the web page shown in **FIGURE A-24**, but the URL that should be at the bottom of the page is torn off. You decide to find the page from the information on the printout. Using Google, search for the page. Create a citation for the page in the MLA format. (Note that the image displayed on the page might differ from the one shown here.) If requested by your instructor, print or save this page of results.

FIGURE A-24

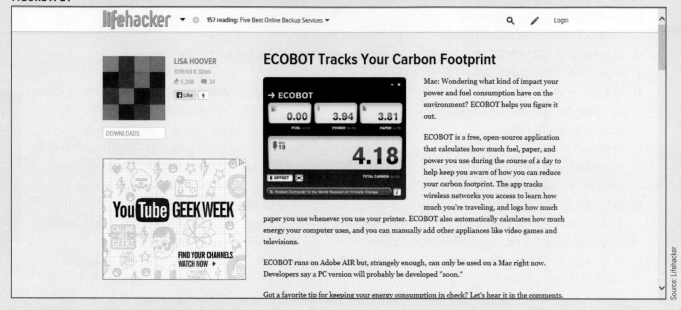

Source: Lifehacker

Constructing Complex Searches

CASE The city planning team requests information on alternative energy-related associations in the region and on alternative energy use in surrounding states and provinces. As you design search strategies, Bob, your friend the reference librarian, provides information on Boolean operators and filters you can use to help refine your searches.

Unit Objectives

After completing this unit, you will be able to:

- Understand Boolean operators
- Narrow a search with the AND operator
- Expand a search with the OR operator
- Restrict a search with the NOT operator
- Use multiple Boolean operators
- Search with filters
- Combine Boolean operators and filters
- Use advanced search operators
- Use metasearch engines

Files You Will Need

No files needed.

Understand Boolean Operators

Learning
Outcomes
• Identify Boolean
  operators
• Illustrate Boolean
  operators with
  Venn diagrams

The English language uses **syntax**, a special set of rules, for combining words to form grammatical sentences. Many search engines allow **complex search queries**, or advanced searches, which use special connecting words and symbols called Boolean operators. Search engines use **Boolean logic**, a special mathematical syntax, to perform complex searches. In Boolean logic, keywords act like nouns in a sentence. Like nouns, keywords represent subjects. You use **Boolean operators**, connecting words such as AND, OR, and NOT, to tell a search engine how to interpret your complex searches. Boolean operators work like conjunctions in a sentence, defining connections between keywords. Boolean logic is usually illustrated with Venn diagrams. **CASE** ▸ *Bob provides information on Boolean operators and on Venn diagrams.*

DETAILS

To review Boolean operators and Venn diagrams:

- **Venn diagrams**

  Venn diagrams are drawings that visually represent searches using Boolean operators. For example, consider the Venn diagrams in **FIGURE B-1**. The rectangle represents the web. Circles inside the rectangle represent groups of related web pages, called **sets**. One circle represents a search for pages containing the word cats. Another circle represents a search for dogs. If the circles overlap, the overlapping area represents pages that are retrieved by both searches. This overlapping area is called the **intersection** of the sets. If you limit your search to pages containing both of the words, the search results are represented by the intersection of these two circles. If you expand your search to pages containing either word, the search results are represented by both full circles. This is called the **union** of the two sets. If you restrict your search to pages containing one word, but not the other one, this search is represented by the part of one circle that does not overlap the other one. This search excludes one set from the other. **TABLE B-1** shows how the searches illustrated by the Venn diagrams are entered and interpreted.

- **Boolean operators**

  Boolean operators, AND, OR, and NOT, expand, narrow, or restrict searches based on Boolean logic. Boolean logic, or Boolean algebra, is the field of mathematics that defines how Boolean operators manipulate large sets of data. Search engines handle large data sets and use Boolean logic to perform complex searches, usually called advanced searches. Boolean operators act as commands to the search engine. How they connect keywords and phrases tells the search engine how to interpret your search and thus helps you retrieve the results you want. Boolean operators control which keywords *must* be on the web page (**AND**), which *may* or *may not* be on the web page (**OR**), and which keyword *must not* be on the web page (**NOT**).

- **Default Boolean operator**

  Search engines insert Boolean operators into multiple word searches whether you supply them in the search query or not. The operator that the engine automatically uses is called the **default operator**. Most search engines default to AND. Others default to OR. When you search two or more words, some engines assume you want the words in a phrase and treat the query as if you used quotation marks. Being aware of an engine's default operator is important to create the best search strategy for that engine.

- **Where to use Boolean operators**

  Some search engines allow Boolean searching on the basic search page, but some allow it only on the advanced search page. In the past, almost all search engines recognized all Boolean operators when typed in all capital letters in the Search text box on the basic search page. Now many only recognize them if you use the advanced search page's specialized text boxes. Some do not allow the use of the English words AND or NOT, but do allow the plus sign (+) or minus sign (–) instead.

FIGURE B-1: Venn diagrams comparing search results for six searches

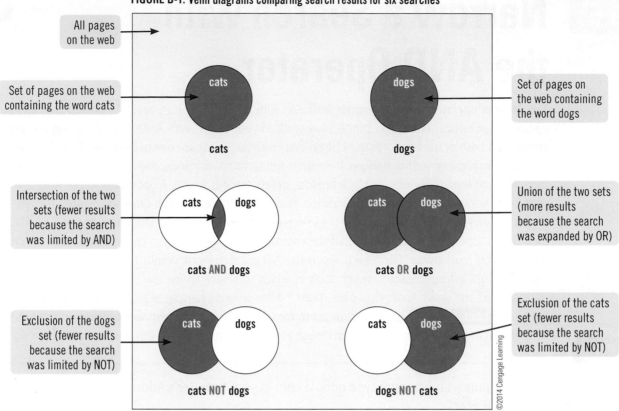

All pages on the web

Set of pages on the web containing the word cats

Set of pages on the web containing the word dogs

Intersection of the two sets (fewer results because the search was limited by AND)

Union of the two sets (more results because the search was expanded by OR)

Exclusion of the dogs set (fewer results because the search was limited by NOT)

Exclusion of the cats set (fewer results because the search was limited by NOT)

cats AND dogs

cats OR dogs

cats NOT dogs

dogs NOT cats

©2014 Cengage Learning

TABLE B-1: How the searches represented in Figure B-1 might be entered in and interpreted by a search engine

search	operator	search interpreted as asking for
cats	*<no operator>*	web pages containing the word *cats*
dogs	*<no operator>*	web pages containing the word *dogs*
cats dogs	AND	web pages containing *both* words (AND is the assumed operator in most search tools, so you rarely type it)
cats OR dogs	OR	web pages containing *either* word
cats NOT dogs	NOT	web pages containing the word *cats* but *not* the word *dogs*
dogs -cats	NOT	web pages containing the word *dogs* but *not* the word *cats*

©2014 Cengage Learning

Remembering Boolean logic

You might remember Boolean logic and Venn diagrams from a math class. An Englishman named George Boole (1815–1864) invented a form of symbolic logic called Boolean algebra, which is used in the fields of mathematics, logic, computer science, and artificial intelligence. John Venn (1843–1923), also an Englishman, used his diagrams to explain visually what Boole had described symbolically—the intersection, union, and exclusion of sets. Little did they know then that they were creating the foundation of the language that Internet search engines use today.

Narrow a Search with the AND Operator

The Boolean operator AND (sometimes indicated with a plus sign) is a powerful operator that limits or narrows your results. When you connect keywords in your search with AND, you are telling the search engine that both of the keywords must be on every web page, not just one or the other. Each AND added to your search query further narrows the search results to fewer pages, and these results pages will be more relevant than those returned by a broader, or less specific, search. A good time to use AND is when your initial keyword or phrase search finds too many irrelevant results. You can also use AND to force the search engine to include a stop word in the search query. Remember that most search engines use AND as their default operator, which means that the engine assumes you mean to connect keywords with AND unless you tell it otherwise. Google actually treats AND as a stop word, despite the capitalization. However, you still might encounter some search tools in which you have to use the plus sign or AND. If you're unsure, check the search tool's Help page. **TABLE B-2** lists several examples of search queries using the AND operator. **CASE** *Bob explains that to search for solar energy associations near Portland, you can use the AND operator to narrow your search, even though you will not type AND between your keywords.*

STEPS

1. **Start your web browser, type google.com in your browser's Address bar, then press [Enter]**

   The Google search form opens. To illustrate how Boolean operators can broaden or narrow a search, first you will search for web pages that contain the phrase *solar energy association*.

2. **Type "solar energy association" in the Search text box, then click the Search button**

   Note the number of results. Now you will search for pages that contain the text *Portland*.

3. **Delete the search query in the Search text box, type portland, then click the Search button**

   Note the number of results. To find the pages that contain both the phrase *"solar energy association"* and the text *Portland*, you would have to read as many web pages as these two sets of results combined. Instead, you can create a search query using a Boolean operator to identify these pages for you.

4. **Delete the search query in the Search text box, type "solar energy association" portland, then click the Search button**

   This search, using the assumed AND operator, narrows your results to *solar energy association* pages that also contain *Portland*. **FIGURE B-2** shows a Venn diagram of this search, and **FIGURE B-3** shows the search results page.

Using the plus sign

The plus sign is useful to prevent a search engine from ignoring a stop word. It also functions like quotation marks around a phrase. Whether using quotation marks around a phrase or the plus sign before a single keyword, you are forcing the search engine to look for a word it would normally ignore. For example, *Henry +I* produces the same results as *"Henry I"*. When you use the plus sign, you must leave a space in front of it, but no space between it and the keyword it is connecting to; for example, *+the goal orr* (used to force inclusion of a stop word) and *music* *+blues +memphis* (used as the Boolean AND). Note that using the plus sign in Google also restricts searches to results that contain the exact keyword you typed. This is because Google automatically applies synonyms or other close matches to keywords. For example, Google will return pages with the keyword *childcare* when you enter *childcare* or *California history* for the query *ca history*. However, if you type the plus symbol in front of a keyword, Google searches only for pages that precisely match the keyword.

FIGURE B-2: Venn diagram illustrating results for *"solar energy association" AND portland*

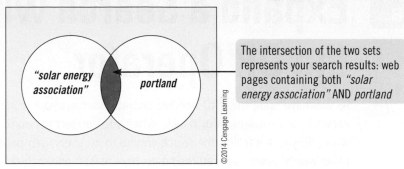

The intersection of the two sets represents your search results: web pages containing both *"solar energy association"* AND *portland*

©2014 Cengage Learning

FIGURE B-3: Google search results for *"solar energy association" AND portland*

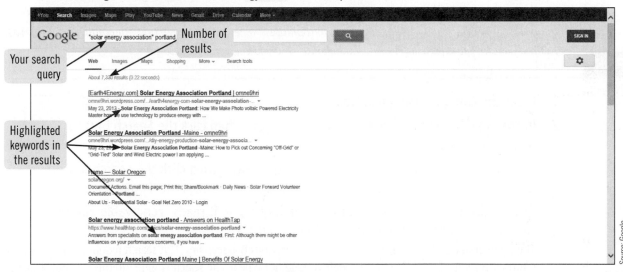

Source: Google

TABLE B-2: Sample search queries using the Boolean operator AND

example	result
solar panels	Assumed AND between keywords returns pages that contain the word *solar* and the word *panels*
"solar panels" "wind turbines"	Assumed AND between search phrases returns pages that contain the phrase *solar panels* and the phrase *wind turbines*
+and i love her	Forces inclusion of the stop word "and"

©2014 Cengage Learning

Keeping a search diary

It is a good idea to log searches as you perform them, noting the Boolean operators used in your search statements, and the number of results returned. This helps you remember what searches you have tried and which ones yielded useful results. Your search logs can also be used by others to reproduce your search results.

Expand a Search with the OR Operator

As you have seen, the AND Boolean operator narrows your search. Conversely, the Boolean operator OR expands, or broadens, your search. When you connect keywords or search phrases in your search query with OR, you are telling the search engine to list every web page that contains any of the keywords. In other words, every page returned must have at least one of the keywords on it but it doesn't need to have more than one. Each OR added to your search expands the search to include more web pages. A good time to use OR is when your initial search finds too few results. Refer to the synonyms or related words you identified when developing your search strategy and connect one or more to your search query with OR. You can also use OR when you want to include more than one spelling of a keyword. **TABLE B-3** lists several examples of search queries using the OR operator. **CASE** *The city planning team requests information on alternative energy sources. Checking your list of synonyms and related words, you decide to perform a complex search using OR to connect the keyword phrases "renewable energy" and "alternative energy". First you will perform searches using the individual phrases so you can compare results.*

STEPS

1. **Clear the** Google Search text box

2. **In the Search text box, type** "renewable energy", **then click the** Search button
   Note the number of results.

3. **Clear the** Search text box, **type** "alternative energy", **then click the** Search button
   Again, note the number of results. Now you will include both search phrases in your search query.

4. **Click in the** Search text box, **edit the search query so it reads** "renewable energy" "alternative energy", **then click the** Search button
   The number of results returned is fewer than the previous two searches. This search requires that every page returned contains both phrases. Although you did not type it, the search engine interpreted your search as if you had connected your phrases with the AND operator. You want to expand your search, not narrow it, so you will connect the phrases with the OR operator.

5. **Click in the** Search text box, **edit the search query so it reads** "renewable energy" OR "alternative energy", **then click the** Search button
   This search requires that every page returned contains only one of your phrases, but not necessarily both. The number of results is greater than the number of results returned when you used the AND operator. **FIGURE B-4** illustrates your search results with a Venn diagram, and **FIGURE B-5** shows the search results page. You might reasonably expect the number of results to equal the sum of your first two searches. However, this is rarely the case because some web pages contain both phrases and the results page eliminates many duplicates.

FIGURE B-4: Venn diagram illustrating results using the Boolean operator OR

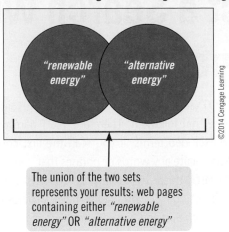

The union of the two sets represents your results: web pages containing either *"renewable energy"* OR *"alternative energy"*

FIGURE B-5: Search results in Google for *"renewable energy"* OR *"alternative energy"*

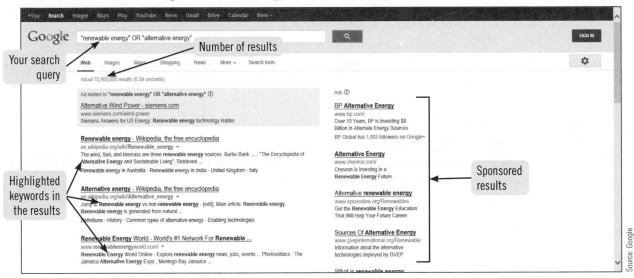

TABLE B-3: Sample search queries using the Boolean operator OR

example	result
oregon **OR** *"pacific northwest"*	Broadens search and returns more results
renewable **OR** *sustainable* **OR** *alternative*	Combines synonyms and returns more results
draft **OR** *draught*	Expands search to include both spellings and returns more results

Restrict a Search with the NOT Operator

The Boolean operator NOT (sometimes indicated with a minus sign, AND NOT, or ANDNOT) excludes the keyword or search phrase that follows it. Therefore, NOT narrows or limits your search by not returning pages that contain the excluded terms. If you scan the first couple of results pages and see numerous irrelevant pages returned, locate any words or phrases that your desired search results should not contain, and then modify your search query by adding these words or phrases with NOT. **TABLE B-4** lists several examples of search queries using NOT. **CASE** *Your search results for solar energy associations in Portland included web pages about both Portland, Oregon, and Portland, Maine. You know that one way to narrow the search would be to use the search phrase "Portland, Oregon". However, you don't want to exclude pages that mention Portland, but don't mention Oregon, so instead, you will use Boolean NOT logic to construct your search query. Before trying NOT, you decide to search without it to compare results.*

STEPS

1. **Clear the** Google Search text box

2. **Type** "solar energy association" portland **in the Search text box, then click the Search button**

   The results include web pages about both Portland, Oregon, and Portland, Maine. Now you want to exclude web pages that contain information about a solar energy association in Portland, Maine. In Google, you must use the minus sign (–) for the Boolean operator NOT.

3. **Click in the** Search text box **immediately after the word** portland, **press [Spacebar], then type** –maine

   Be sure not to leave a space between the minus sign and the word *maine*. When using the minus sign (–), there must always be a space before it and no space between it and the next keyword.

4. **Click the** Search button

   FIGURE B-6 shows a Venn diagram of your search, and **FIGURE B-7** shows the search results page. Note that none of the results pages include the word *Maine*.

FIGURE B-6: Venn diagram illustrating results for the search *"solar energy association"* AND *portland* NOT *maine*

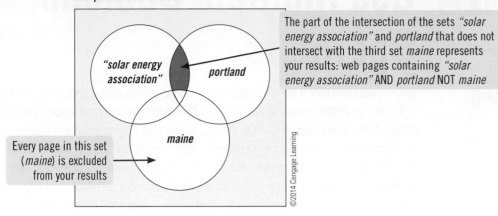

The part of the intersection of the sets *"solar energy association"* and *portland* that does not intersect with the third set *maine* represents your results: web pages containing *"solar energy association"* AND *portland* NOT *maine*

Every page in this set (*maine*) is excluded from your results

©2014 Cengage Learning

FIGURE B-7: Search results in Google for *"solar energy association"* AND *portland* NOT *maine*

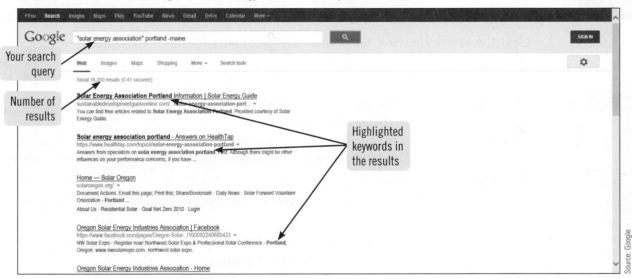

Source: Google

TABLE B-4: Sample search queries using the Boolean operator NOT

example	result
"alternative energy" –geothermal	Returns fewer results because the keyword *geothermal* is excluded
cardinals –"st. louis" –arizona –catholic	Excludes nonrelevant contexts from results

©2014 Cengage Learning

Constructing Complex Searches

Use Multiple Boolean Operators

When you construct a search query with only keywords and phrases, search engines process it from left to right. For example, imagine you want to find information about hybrid cars or electric cars. If you simply entered the query *cars hybrid OR electric*, the search engine would first process *cars AND hybrid* and then process the keyword *electric* separately, thus returning search results about *hybrid cars* or the pages containing the keyword *electric*, not the desired information about hybrid cars or electric cars. To solve this problem, you can use parentheses to control the order in which a query is processed. In our example, enclosing part of the search query in parentheses—*cars AND (hybrid OR electric)*—causes the search engine to pair *cars AND hybrid* as well as cars *AND electric*, giving your desired search results. Using parentheses can have a significant impact on search results. **FIGURE B-8** illustrates results in which the search tool read the query and performed the search from left to right, producing irrelevant results. **FIGURE B-9** illustrates results in which the order of operation was forced using parentheses, producing relevant results. See **TABLE B-5** for steps to use in planning a complex search for alternative energy in British Columbia or Alberta, Canada, excluding pages that mention geothermal energy. **CASE** *In your last team meeting, you agreed to find information on solar energy resources from the surrounding region, not just in Portland, Oregon. Bob suggests you combine Boolean operators to construct a complex search query.*

STEPS

1. **Clear the Search text box, type "solar energy", then click the Search button**

   The search results appear listing web pages that include the search phrase *solar energy*. Now you want to create a search query that finds web pages that contain references to the region surrounding Portland, Oregon.

QUICK TIP
If you had used only the keyword *Washington* in your search query, your results would contain many pages referring to Washington, D.C. Including the word *state* in the search phrase returns results for only the state of Washington.

2. **Clear the Search text box, type "Washington state" OR "British Columbia" OR "Pacific Northwest", then click the Search button**

   The search results appear listing web pages that include the three search phrases in your search query. Now you need to combine and limit these results to web pages about solar energy that also refer to the Northwest.

3. **Clear the Search text box**

   You need to clear the Search text box because Google ignores parentheses added to an executed search query.

4. **In the Search text box, type "solar energy" ("Washington state" OR "British Columbia" OR "Pacific Northwest"), then click the Search button**

   The results list web pages that include the search phrase *solar energy* and at least one of the search phrases between the parentheses. Now you need to modify the search so the results do not include Oregon.

QUICK TIP
Be sure to leave no space between the minus sign and the keyword to be excluded.

5. **Click in the Search text box, edit your search to read "solar energy" ("Washington state" OR "British Columbia" OR "Pacific Northwest") –Oregon, then click the Search button**

   Now the results do not include pages that contain *Oregon*. **FIGURE B-10** illustrates the results.

Using multiple Boolean operators instead of advanced search forms

Most search tools contain advanced search pages, which can be convenient for performing complex searches. If you ever find yourself unsure about what to do when using these pages, return to these basic steps: identifying keywords and related words; sketching Venn diagrams to recall how the Boolean operators work; and writing down your search query using the Boolean operators AND, OR, and NOT. Understanding Boolean logic helps you create successful online search strategies when you use the convenience of advanced search pages. However, the more complex your searches become, the more likely you will need to go back to the basic search page where you have more control over your search statement, thus reducing the chances of inadvertent logic errors.

FIGURE B-8: Venn diagram illustrating the search: *constitution AND American OR "United States"*

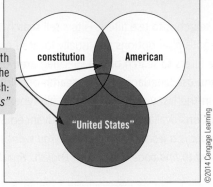

Order of operation was not forced with parentheses, so the search engine read the operators from left to right, resulting in the search: *constitution* AND *American* OR *"United States"*

©2014 Cengage Learning

FIGURE B-9: Venn diagram illustrating the search: *constitution AND (American OR "United States")*

Order of operation was forced with parentheses, so the search engine read inside the parentheses first, resulting in the search: *constitution (American* OR *"United States")*

©2014 Cengage Learning

FIGURE B-10: Venn diagram illustrating the search *"solar energy" AND ("Washington state" OR "British Columbia" OR "Pacific Northwest") NOT Oregon*

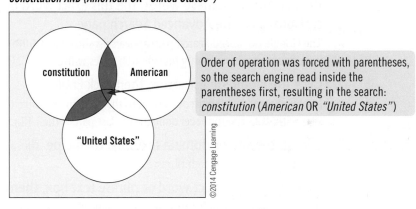

Web pages containing *"solar energy"*

Web pages containing (*"Washington state"* OR *"British Columbia"* OR *"Pacific Northwest"*) AND *"solar energy"* NOT *Oregon*

Web pages containing *Oregon*, which are then excluded from the search results

Web pages containing *"Washington state"* OR *"British Columbia"* OR *"Pacific Northwest"*

©2014 Cengage Learning

TABLE B-5: Planning a complex search with multiple Boolean operators

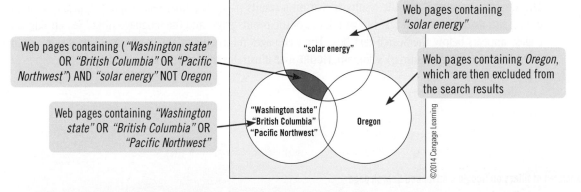

step	example
1. Identify the first concept. Use keywords, synonyms, and related words. Connect them with OR and surround them with parentheses.	(British Columbia OR BC OR Alberta)
2. Identify the second concept. Use keywords, synonyms, and related words. Connect them with OR and surround them with parentheses.	(Canada OR Canadian)
3. Identify the third concept. Quotation marks identify this as a phrase.	"alternative energy"
4. Identify the fourth concept. You want this word excluded from your results, so you use the Boolean operator NOT.	–geothermal
5. Connect all of your concepts into one search statement.	(British Columbia OR BC OR Alberta) AND (Canada OR Canadian) AND "alternative energy" –geothermal

©2014 Cengage Learning

Search with Filters

Learning Outcomes
• Identify search filter options
• Search using a language filter
• Filter search results by domain

Another way to refine a search is to use filters. Filters tell search tools to screen out specified types of web pages or files. A search tool's filter options are usually located on advanced search pages. As you develop your search strategy, use filters to search only a specified area of the web or to exclude specified areas of the web. For example, you use language filters to search only for pages in English, or date filters to search only for pages updated in the last year, or for certain file types such as images, audio, or video. **TABLE B-6** lists examples of filter options available on Google's Advanced Search page. **CASE** ▶ *One of your team members read that Denmark is a leader in wind power. You want to view some Danish sites, but because you don't read Danish, you need to find pages that are in English. You decide to search using filters.*

STEPS

1. **Scroll to the bottom of the Google search results page, click the Advanced search link, then clear the all these words, the this exact word or phrase, and the any of these words text boxes on the Advanced Search page**

   The Google Advanced Search page appears, as shown in **FIGURE B-11**. First, you want to set up a filter so that your search results will only include web pages written in English.

2. **Click the language list arrow, then click English**

   Now you want to restrict your search to the domain exclusive to Denmark, that is, web pages stored on web sites with *dk* as the top-level domain (the last part of the URL).

3. **Click in the site or domain text box, then type .dk**

   Now you can type a search phrase.

4. **Click in the this exact word or phrase text box, then type wind power**

   In the Advanced Search form, you do not need to type the search phrase within quotation marks. This specialized text box interprets any words typed here as a phrase, so quotation marks are assumed.

5. **Click Advanced Search**

   The search is executed and the results appear on a results page. The final search query appears as *"wind power" site:.dk* in the Search text box at the top of the results page, and the language filter "Search English pages" appears below the Search text box. The web pages returned contain the phrase *wind power*, are in English, and are from Denmark's domain. **FIGURE B-12** illustrates the results in a Venn diagram.

TABLE B-6: Examples of filters on Google's Advanced Search page

filter	what it does
Language	Limits search to pages written in a specified language (English, French, etc.)
File type	Limits search to pages in a specified format (.pdf, .xls, .doc, .ppt, etc.)
Last update	Limits search to pages updated, crawled, and indexed in a specified time period (1 day, 1 week, 1 month, etc.)
Site or domain	Limits search to pages only with a specified domain or within a specified site
Terms appearing	Limits search to pages containing your keywords in a specified location (URL, title, text, links on the page, etc.)
Usage rights	Limits search to pages you are free to use (still check usage rights for each page)
Region	Limits search to pages originating from a specified region or country (not all URLs identify a country)
Numbers ranging from	Limits search to pages containing numbers in a specified range

©2014 Cengage Learning

FIGURE B-11: Boolean logic and filters on Google's Advanced Search form

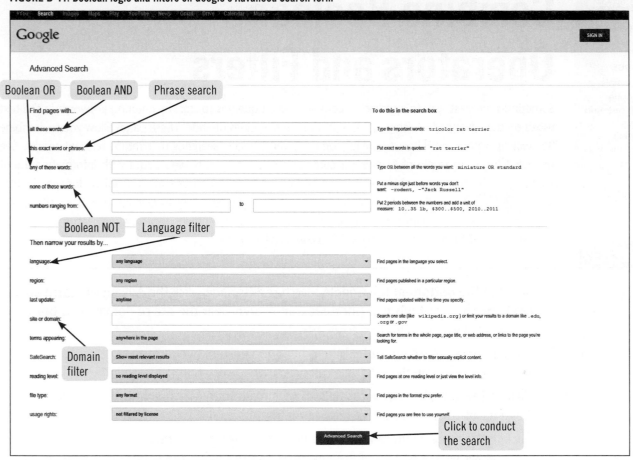

Source: Google

FIGURE B-12: Venn diagram illustrating results for
"wind power" AND domain:.dk AND language: English

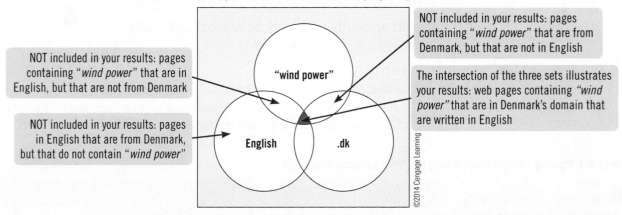

NOT included in your results: pages containing *"wind power"* that are in English, but that are not from Denmark

NOT included in your results: pages in English that are from Denmark, but that do not contain *"wind power"*

NOT included in your results: pages containing *"wind power"* that are from Denmark, but that are not in English

The intersection of the three sets illustrates your results: web pages containing *"wind power"* that are in Denmark's domain that are written in English

©2014 Cengage Learning

Filtering domains in the URL

When you apply a domain filter, the search is restricted to URLs hosted in the specified domain as indicated by the letters after the period in the URL. Most web sites in the United States have URLs that end in three letters that represent the type of organization hosting the web site. For example, university sites end in .edu, government sites end in .gov, commercial sites end in .com, and nonprofits end in .org. Others include .biz, .pro, .info, and .net. In addition, .us, .coop, .museum, and .name are available. Many web sites located in other countries use two-letter country codes: Canada's domain is .ca; the United Kingdom's domain is .uk; and Japan's domain is .jp. Any of these codes can limit search results when using a domain filter. For a listing of top-level domains, including two-letter country codes, go to www.iana.org/domains/root/db.

Combine Boolean Operators and Filters

Learning Outcomes
- Plan a complex search using Boolean operators and filters
- Search using Boolean operators and filters

Sometimes the best way to approach a complex search query is to start by entering keywords in the text boxes on the advanced search pages that most search engines provide. These pages allow you to combine Boolean operators and filters to create complex, very specific searches that return relevant results. See **TABLE B-7** for an example of planning a complex search to identify web pages with information about alternative energies other than geothermal stored on web sites from the Canadian domain, in PDF format. **CASE** ▸ *As discussed with your city planning team, you want to identify some university-related Canadian pages on alternative energies. You don't need pages on geothermal energy and because they will be easy to print and share, you want pages that are in a PDF format.*

STEPS

1. **Scroll to the bottom of the Google search results page, click the** Advanced search link, **clear the** this exact word or phrase text box, **then clear the** site or domain text box
   English is still selected in the language list box.

2. **Click in the** all these words **text box, then type** university energy
   This text box represents the AND Boolean operator.

3. **Click in the** any of these words text box, **type** alternative sustainable renewable
   This text box represents the OR Boolean operator.

4. **Click in the** none of these words text box, **then type** geothermal
   This text box represents the NOT Boolean operator. Next, you want to restrict the results to web pages located in the .ca domain—the domain for Canada.

5. **Click in the** site or domain text box, **then type** .ca
   Finally, you want to filter the results so that only pages in PDF format appear.

6. **Click the** file type list arrow, **then click** Adobe Acrobat PDF (.pdf)
   Compare your settings with those shown in **FIGURE B-13**.

7. **Click** Advanced Search
   The complete search query *university energy alternative OR sustainable OR renewable –geothermal site:.ca filetype:pdf* appears in the Search text box at the top of the search results page, and only English pages were searched. A quick check of the search results verifies that the Boolean text boxes and the filters worked as you expected.

TABLE B-7: Planning a complex search using both Boolean operators and filters

step	example
1. Identify the first concept. Connect keywords with **OR** and surround them with parentheses.	(alternative OR renewable OR sustainable)
2. Identify the second concept. Use keywords/synonyms/ related words, connect them with **OR**, then surround them with parentheses.	(energy OR energies)
3. Identify the third concept.	–geothermal
4. Use filters as needed.	Language: English Domain: .ca File Format: .pdf
5. Create the final search query.	(alternative OR renewable OR sustainable) (energy OR energies) –geothermal site:.ca file type:.pdf lang:.eng

©2014 Cengage Learning

FIGURE B-13: Using Boolean logic and filters on Google's Advanced Search form

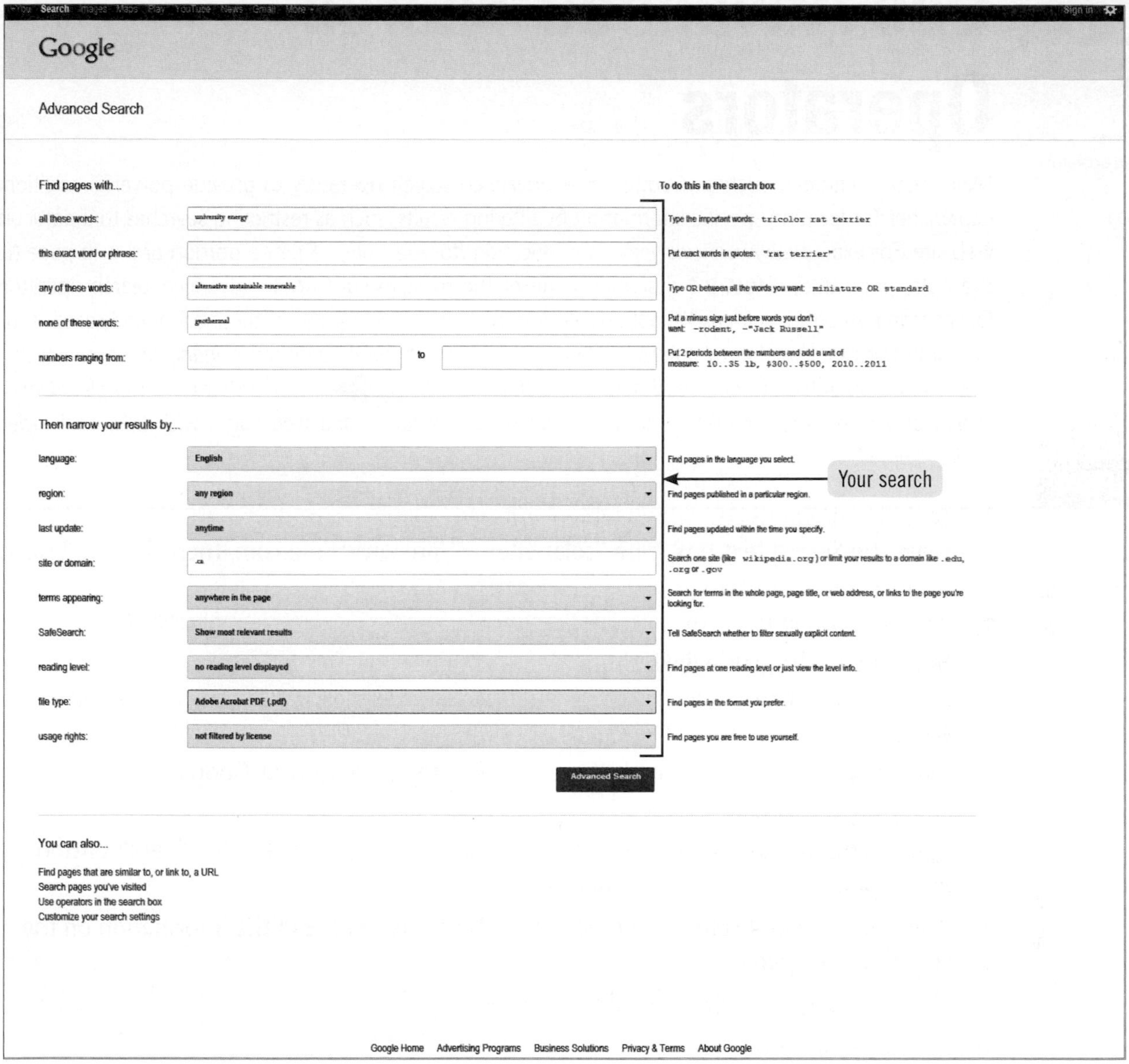

Source: Google

Using the search text boxes on an advanced search page

When using advanced search text boxes, you do not actually type the Boolean operators. When using these specialized text boxes, the search engine understands the operator you want to use, so you can enter multiple words without the operators. However, if you need to enter a phrase in an OR box, you need to include quotation marks around the phrase. For example, to search for *solar panels OR wind turbines* on Google's Advanced Search page, enter: "solar panels" and "wind turbines" in the any of these words text box. This ensures your search is interpreted as two phrases. This is an example of why, when your complex searches get more complicated, as with multiple phrases or more than three keywords separated by OR, it is often preferable to go back to the basic search form.

Use Advanced Search Operators

Major search engines, such as Google, offer advanced search operators to provide powerful additional capabilities for locating specific information by filtering results, such as restricting searches to a particular web site (for example, www.newsweek.com), location (for example, UK), or a portion of a web page (for example, page title). **TABLE B-8** describes some of the most useful Google advanced search operators. Other search engines, such as Yahoo! and Microsoft Bing, support some of these advanced search tools, although the exact operator might be different; for example, the Bing operator *inanchor:* corresponds to the Google operator *allinanchor:* described in **TABLE B-8**. **CASE** ▶ *You decide to use Google advanced search operators to locate relevant articles in an online magazine and web pages with titles that include "solar energy."*

STEPS

1. **Clear the** Search text box, **type** "solar energy" site:www.time.com, **then click the** Search button

   A list of articles on Time.com containing the phrase "*solar energy*" appears, similar to **FIGURE B-14**.

2. **Click one of the article links, then briefly examine the information**

   After looking at the magazine article, you are ready to search for more web pages that contain information about solar energy. You decide to search for pages containing *solar energy* in the web page title.

3. **Click the** Back button **in your browser window to return to your Google search results page**

4. **Clear the** Search text box, **type** allintitle:"solar energy", **then click the** Search button

   A list of results appears, as shown in **FIGURE B-15**.

5. **Examine the list of results, then click one of the links and read the information on the resulting web page**

   The web page should contain relevant information.

TABLE B-8: Examples of Google Advanced Search operators

operator	allows you to	example
allinanchor:	Locate pages based on the keywords used to link to them from other pages	allinanchor:useful solar energy sites—Finds pages that are called useful solar energy sites by other web sites
allintext:	Locate pages containing all keywords	allintext:consultant renewable energy—Finds consultants in renewable energy
allintitle:	Locate pages with titles that contain all keywords	allintitle:wind power—Finds pages with titles containing wind power
allinurl:	Locate pages with all keywords appearing in their URLs (web addresses)	allinurl:alternative energy—Finds pages containing alternative energy in the URL
site:	Search a specific web site based on keywords	solar energy site:www.newsweek.com—Finds articles about solar energy on the Newsweek web site
define:	Locate definitions for words and phrases on the Internet	define:alternative energy—Finds definitions for alternative energy
info:	Locate information about a specified page	info:www.eere.energy.gov—Finds information about the U.S. Department of Energy web site
link:	Locate pages that point to a specific URL	link:www.eere.energy.gov—Finds pages that link to the U.S. Department of Energy web site

©2014 Cengage Learning

FIGURE B-14: Search results using Google's *site:* operator

site: operator in the search query

Sponsored results are not filtered

Results all appear on pages on Time.com

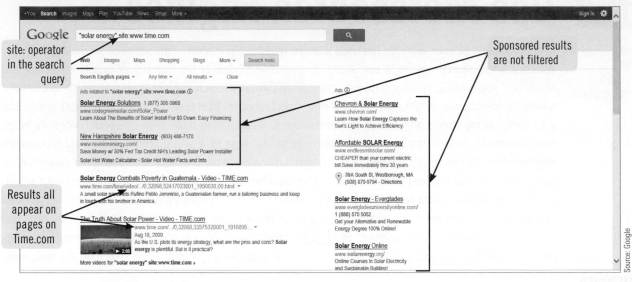

FIGURE B-15: Search results using Google's *allintitle:* operator

allintitle: operator in the search query

Results have *solar energy* in the page title

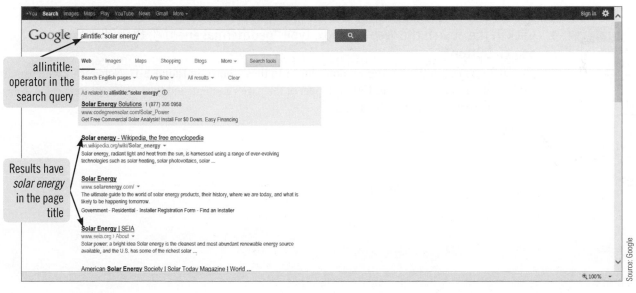

Constructing Complex Searches

Use Metasearch Engines

Until now, each of your searches has used a single search engine. Even with complex searching, you only search a single search engine. If one search engine doesn't deliver the number or quality of results you need, or if you want to quickly compare results from different search engines to decide which to use for a particular search, you might want to try a metasearch engine. **Metasearch engines** do not search the web itself; rather, they search search engines' indexes. By searching more than one search engine's index simultaneously, metasearch engines access more of the web in a single search. However, metasearch engines often do not search the best search engines, because of the fees such search engines charge. Also, search engines that are busy with too many other searches at the exact moment you conduct your search are sometimes skipped, so results can be inconsistent. Metasearch results are broad, but often not as deep as a single search engine's. Metasearching is a good place to start when you want to check the first few results from several search engines. **CASE** ▶ *While searching for information on alternative energy resources, you have become intrigued with geothermal energy. Bob suggests a simple search on this topic using a metasearch engine.*

STEPS

1. **Type metacrawler.com in your browser's Address bar, then press [Enter]**

   The MetaCrawler search form appears in your browser window.

2. **Click in the Search text box, type "geothermal energy", then click SEARCH**

   Your search is now simultaneously sent to multiple search engines, and the results page appears in your browser window, as shown in **FIGURE B-16**. Notice that if the result came from a sponsored result, the word "Sponsored" appears at the end of its URL. You want to try another metasearch engine.

3. **Type excite.com in your browser's Address bar, then press [Enter]**

   The Excite search form appears in your browser window.

4. **Click in the Search the Web text box, type "geothermal energy", then click the Search button**

   The results appear in the browser window, similar to those shown in **FIGURE B-17**. Note each Excite search result contains the page title, its URL, a snippet of the page's content, and the sources the item came from, including search engines and directories.

Maximizing metasearching

To effectively use a metasearch engine always read its Help pages to determine how "smart" the engine is in translating specific search commands into queries that other search engines understand. With this information, you can learn if you need to use quotation marks to indicate a phrase. If you're not sure how smart the metasearch engine is, use simple searches consisting of only a few keywords. Also, because the search engines used by a metasearch engine change regularly, note which engines are being used when you perform your search and which are returning the most useful results.

FIGURE B-16: Search results for *"geothermal energy"* in MetaCrawler

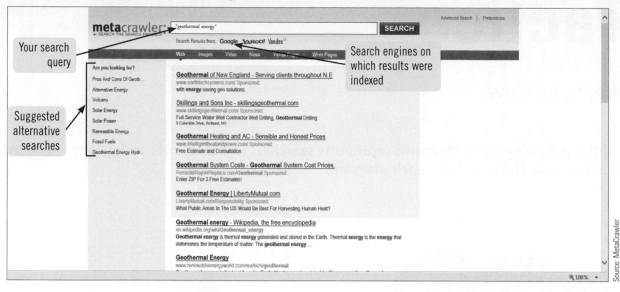

FIGURE B-17: Search results for *"geothermal energy"* in Excite

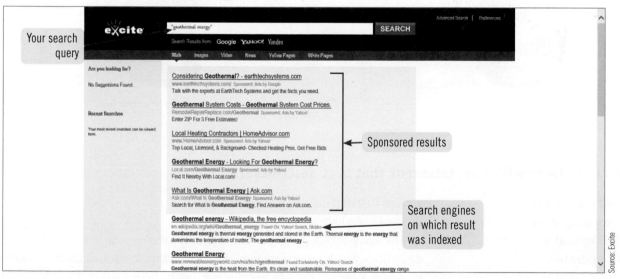

Constructing Complex Searches

Practice

Concepts Review

Each of the following Venn diagrams represents searches. The blue color represents the search results. Write out the search for each diagram.

FIGURE B-18

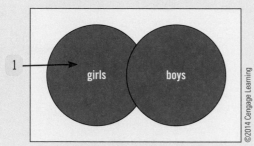

FIGURE B-20

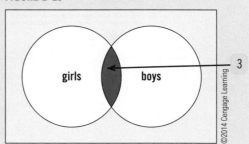

FIGURE B-19

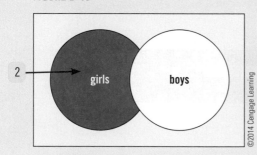

FIGURE B-21

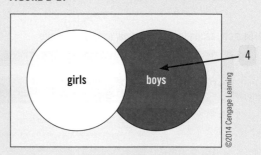

Match each term with the statement that best describes it.

5. **Boolean operators**
6. **Venn diagrams**
7. **AND operator**
8. **OR operator**
9. **NOT operator**
10. **Metasearch engine**
11. **Parentheses**
12. **Filters**
13. **Default operator**

a. Aids to screen out unwanted web pages
b. Used to exclude words from a search query
c. The operator that the engine automatically uses
d. Indicate how keywords are to relate to each other in a search query
e. A search engine that searches multiple search engines rather than the web itself
f. A way to visualize how Boolean operators work
g. One way to narrow a search
h. Used to connect synonyms
i. Force the order of operation in a Boolean search

Select the best answer from the list of choices.

14. **The place where two search results sets overlap is called the _____ of the two sets.**
    a. intersection
    b. union
    c. margin
    d. combination

15. **When you use the Boolean operator AND to link another keyword to your search query, you find _____.**
    a. exactly the same number of web pages
    b. more web pages
    c. fewer web pages
    d. None of the above

16. **Equivalent wording for the Boolean OR in an advanced search list box might be _____.**
    a. must not contain
    b. either of the words
    c. all of the words
    d. none of the words

17. **Which is not a standard variation of the Boolean operator NOT?**
    a. AND NOT
    b. NOT MORE
    c. The hyphen or minus sign (–)
    d. ANDNOT

18. **Which is not a potential downside to using metasearch engines?**
    a. Usually limited to simple searches
    b. Don't search the best search engines
    c. Instability
    d. Inconsistency

19. **If the order of operation in a complex Boolean search is not forced, the search tool _____.**
    a. automatically applies filters to your search
    b. reads the query from left to right
    c. inserts the parentheses for you
    d. returns no search results

20. **A search tool that doesn't recognize Boolean operators as English words in its basic search _____.**
    a. cannot be used to search with Boolean logic
    b. sometimes allows the Boolean AND and NOT if you use the plus sign (+) and the minus sign (–) instead of words
    c. probably allows Boolean searching from text boxes or list boxes in its advanced search pages
    d. both b and c

21. **The part of a URL that can contain a two-letter country code is the _____.**
    a. file
    b. page
    c. file extension
    d. domain

22. **Which is *not* true of metasearch engines?**
    a. They search other search engines' indexes.
    b. They might skip searching an engine they normally search if that engine is busy at that moment.
    c. Their results are always as deep as individual search engines.
    d. They are a good place to start when you want to see the top results from several engines.

23. Using parentheses in a complex search tells the search engine that _____.
   a. the words inside the parentheses should be treated as a subset in the search
   b. the part of the search inside the parentheses should be performed first
   c. the words inside the parentheses should be excluded from the search
   d. both a and b

Skills Review

If requested by your instructor, create a document listing the answers to the questions asked in the following exercises.

1. **Understand Boolean operators.**
   a. Describe the effects on search results when you use the Boolean operator AND.
   b. Describe the effects on search results when you use the Boolean operator OR.
   c. Describe the effects on search results when you use the Boolean operator NOT.
   d. What symbol can you use instead of the Boolean operator AND?
   e. What symbol can you use instead of the Boolean operator NOT?

2. **Narrow a search with the AND operator.**
   a. Go to the Google basic search form.
   b. Perform an initial search on **energy**, and note the number of results.
   c. Edit your search query by adding **green** to it, run the search, and then note the number of results.
   d. Modify your search query again by adding **solutions**. Run the search, and then note the number of results.
   e. How did the number of results change after each search (in other words, did the number increase or decrease)? Why?

3. **Expand a search with the OR operator.**
   a. Return to your initial search for **energy**.
   b. Modify your search query by adding **OR renewable**, run the search, and then note the number of results.
   c. Modify your search query again by adding **OR technologies**, run the search, and then note the number of results.
   d. How did adding each OR statement affect the number of results? Why?

4. **Restrict a search with the NOT operator.**
   a. Return to your initial search for **energy**.
   b. Modify your search query by adding **–renewable**, run the search, and then note the number of results.
   c. Modify your search query again by adding **–technologies**, run the search, and then note the number of results.
   d. How did adding each NOT statement affect the number of results? Why?

5. **Use multiple Boolean operators.**
   a. Clear the Google Search text box, and then perform a search using the search query **energy green OR renewable**. Note the number of results.
   b. Clear the Google Search text box, and then retype the search query from step a, but this time enclose **green OR renewable** in parentheses. Run the search again. Note the number of results.
   c. How did adding the parentheses affect the number of results?
   d. Clear the Google Search text box, and then retype the search query from step b, but modify it by adding **(solutions OR technologies)** to the search criteria. Run the search, and then note the number of results.
   e. How did adding each of the multiple Boolean operators affect the number of results? Why?

Skills Review (continued)

6. **Search with filters.**

   a. Clear the Google Search text box, click the Advanced search link, and then clear the text boxes on the Advanced Search page of any search criteria.

   b. Enter text in the appropriate text box or boxes on the Advanced Search page to create the search query **energy green OR renewable**.

   c. Run the search, and note the number of search results.

   d. Return to the Advanced Search page, and then add a filter for web pages written in English, a filter for web pages modified and indexed in the past year, and a filter for pages with the domain **.org**.

   e. Run the search, and note the number of search results.

   f. What was the final search query (including any labels that identify the filters applied)?

7. **Combine Boolean operators and filters.**

   a. Clear the Google Advanced Search text boxes and filters.

   b. Enter text in the appropriate text box or boxes on the Advanced Search page to create the search query **energy efficient renewable**.

   c. Enter text in the appropriate text box or boxes on the Advanced Search page to add the search phrase **"department of energy"** to the search query.

   d. Run the search, and note the number of search results.

   e. Return to the Advanced Search page, and then add a filter for web pages written in English, a filter for pages modified and indexed in the past year, and a filter for pages with the domain **.net**.

   f. Run the search, and note the number of search results.

   g. What was the final search query (including any labels that identify the filters applied)?

8. **Use advanced search operators.**

   a. Go to the Google basic search form.

   b. Create a search query using the appropriate advanced search operator to search for **renewable energy** only on the web site www.washingtonpost.com.

   c. Run the search. If requested by your instructor, print or save this page of results.

   d. Explore one of the articles on the Time magazine web site.

   e. Return to the Google search page, and then clear the Search text box.

   f. Create a search query using the appropriate advanced search operator to find web pages that have the exact phrase **"renewable energy"** in **the page title**.

   g. Run the search. If requested by your instructor, print or save this page of results.

   h. Explore one of the links to see if the result is relevant.

9. **Use metasearch engines.**

   a. Go to the WebCrawler metasearch engine at **webcrawler.com**.

   b. Perform an initial search using the search query **"green energy"**. If requested by your instructor, print or save this page of results.

   c. Go to the Excite metasearch engine at **excite.com**.

   d. Repeat the search at this web site. Note the number of results. If requested by your instructor, print or save this page of results.

Independent Challenge 1

If requested by your instructor, create a document listing the answer to the question asked in the following exercises.

You want to find web sites in Spain (domain .es) about the Picasso Museum in Barcelona. You don't read Spanish, so you want the web pages to be in English.

- **a.** Use the Google Advanced Search page to set the appropriate filters, and then perform your search.
- **b.** Modify the search query to include only web pages in PDF format.
- **c.** Run the search again. Examine the search results.
- **d.** Go to the Excite metasearch engine at **Excite.com**. Click Search (without typing anything in the Search the Web text box), and then click the Advanced Search link next in the upper right corner of the page. Repeat the search you performed in step a using the Excite Advanced Search form. Compare the results with the results you received when you used Google. Are any of the results on the first page of results from Excite the same as the results on the first page of results from Google?

Independent Challenge 2

If requested by your instructor, create a document listing the answers to the questions asked in the following exercises.

You need to find something to help you create a personal budget. You want to consider both software and tools that you can fill out by hand.

- **a.** Go to the Google basic search form, create a search query, and then perform your search.
- **b.** Scroll through the first page of results.
- **c.** At the bottom of the results page, click one of the suggested search query links that appears under the "Searches related to…" heading. Examine the first page in this set of results. Which set of results seems to be more relevant?
- **d.** Go to the WebCrawler metasearch engine at **webcrawler.com**. Using the search query that produced the most relevant results, conduct that search, and then examine the results. Are they the same as the Google results?
- **e.** Go to the Dogpile metasearch engine at **dogpile.com**, and then perform the same search. Once again, examine the results and compare them to the Google and MetaCrawler results.
- **f.** Which search engine do you think returned the most relevant results?

Independent Challenge 3

If requested by your instructor, create a document listing the answers to the questions asked in the following exercises.

In our increasingly long-lived society, the number of career changes over a lifetime continues to grow. Fortunately, the Internet provides a wealth of information on how to choose a career, with everything from career-path quizzes to professional advice. You decide to avail yourself of these resources to find out how to chart a career.

- **a.** Conduct a search on Google using the search query **choose career**. Examine the results.
- **b.** Broaden your search by adding multiple Boolean operators so that the search query includes the following synonyms for the word *choose*: *pick, select,* and *find*. (*Hint*: Make sure you use the Boolean operator that broadens your results, not narrows them.) Examine your results.
- **c.** Modify your search query again to exclude career quizzes and tests from the results (because you are looking for advice only). Examine your results.
- **d.** Modify your search again so that the results include pages that are specific to a career that you are interested in. Examine your results.

Independent Challenge 4: Explore

If requested by your instructor, create a document listing the answers to the questions asked in the following exercises.

You and some friends want to go on an ecotour (an ecologically friendly vacation). You are interested in tours to Central and South America, but you need the information to be in English.

    a. Consider your search query, and think of synonyms and related words.

    b. Construct a search query, and then run the search using the Google basic search form.

    c. Modify your search query by adding multiple Boolean operators and using parentheses to look for ecotours that include volunteer work or community development as part of the tour. What is your final search query?

    d. Examine your results, and then identify a web site that seems to have tours that meet your needs. Run a new search that searches for pages with links that point to the web site you identified. (*Hint*: Use the link: operator.) What is your final search query?

    e. You want to find an ecotour in Costa Rica or Patagonia that focuses on the rainforest or wildlife, and you need the results to be in English. Go to the Google basic search page, and then type a complex search query in the Search text box. Run the search, and then examine your results. Modify the query as needed to get relevant results.

    f. Open a new tab or browser window, go to the Google Advanced Search page, and then try to use the form to create your search query. Run the search, and then examine your results.

    g. Which search, the basic or the advanced, provided the best results? Was it easier to construct your specific search query using the basic or the advanced search form?

Visual Workshop

Construct a search query on Bing using the basic search form to find the web page shown in **FIGURE B-22**. This page is stored on the NASA web site. Your query should be precise enough so this page is one of the first few results. If requested by your instructor, print or save the page on which this photo is displayed.

FIGURE B-22

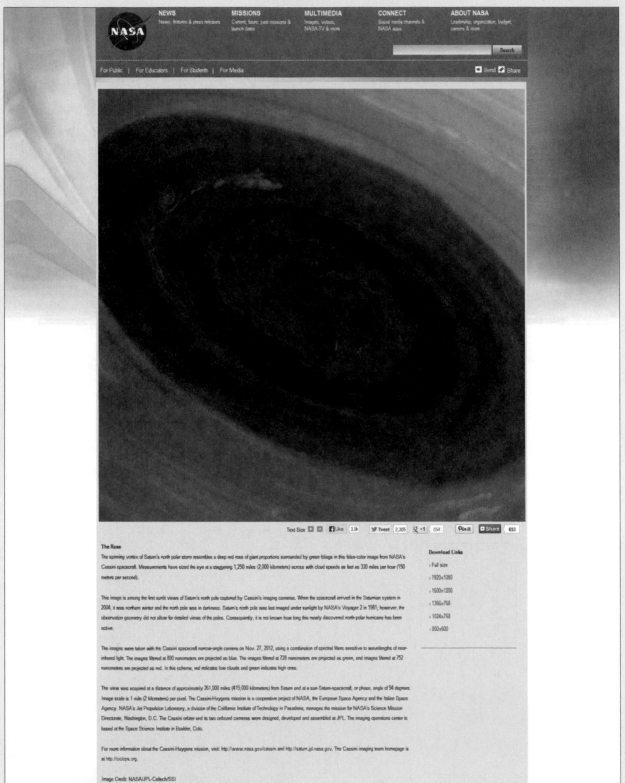

Finding Specialty Information

CASE You will be attending a conference on renewable energy in Washington, D.C. In preparing for this conference, you speak with Bob Johnson, the reference librarian, who suggests you continue your research on alternative energy using specialty search engines and subject directories.

Unit Objectives

After completing this unit, you will be able to:

- Understand subject guides
- Use a subject guide
- Understand the deep web
- Search periodical databases
- Find places

- Find people and businesses
- Use a specialized search engine
- Find online reference sources
- Find government information

Files You Will Need

No files needed.

Understand Subject Guides

Subject guides, also known as **subject directories**, **Internet directories**, and **subject trees**, are indexed web pages that can be either automatically generated by computer algorithms or hand-compiled and maintained by people. They tend to be organized alphabetically and hierarchically by topic. Some search engines provide computer generated subject guides and most hand-compiled subject guides provide the ability to search their catalogue of information. However, hand-compiled subject guides are often prepared by field experts and reference librarians, using carefully selected criteria to determine the most appropriate resources to include in them. Hence, hand-compiled subject guides typically offer users greater selectivity and quality of information but less coverage than computer generated subject guides. **TABLE C-1** lists several subject guides. **CASE** *You want to become more efficient at searching the web for reliable information on alternative energy, so you decide to learn more about subject guides.*

DETAILS

FIGURE C-1 and **FIGURE C-2** illustrate the following notable characteristics of subject guides:

• **Organization**

Subject guides organize links to web sites into topical hierarchies. A **hierarchy** is a ranked order. The ranked order typically goes from more general to more specific. For example, the general topics or categories (in bold) in the Open Directory Project subject guide, shown in **FIGURE C-1**, are followed by related, more specific topics, or subcategories. Clicking a topic, such as Science, links to a list of subtopics. Subtopics link to increasingly detailed topics. You navigate or browse a subject guide primarily by "**drilling down**," or clicking through topics and subtopics arranged hierarchically, under increasingly specific subject headings.

• **Selectivity**

 Subject guides are selective. In better subject guides, qualified people rather than computer programs decide which web pages are worthy of inclusion. Subject guides can provide links to useful sites that search engine spiders are unable to access. They often include web pages with links to other sites covering all aspects of a topic. Subject experts also include sites that might cover one or two very detailed subtopics. This kind of selectivity ensures that returned web pages are some of the best on the subject. Because of this selectivity, subject guides are relatively small, which can be an advantage, saving you the time and trouble of sifting through thousands of search engine results.

• **Accessibility**

In addition to hierarchical lists of topics, better subject guides provide search forms with which you can use keywords to search the indexed web pages. A subject guide might also provide its lists of topics arranged in multiple ways, such as listing topics alphabetically, geographically, chronologically, or by the Dewey Decimal subject classification system.

QUICK TIP
Annotations are
great time-savers, as
they provide expert
previews of sites
for you.

• **Annotations**

Annotations are summaries or reviews of the contents of a web page, written by the subject guide contributors, usually experts in the field, such as professionals or academics, or experts in information and the web, such as librarians. Annotations make subject guides the tools of choice for many researchers.

• **Relevant results**

 Subject guides return fewer results than search engines, but the results are more likely to be reliable and useful. As shown in **FIGURE C-2**, typical subject guide results pages include the number of results, an annotation for each result, and topics under which related sites are indexed. The latter can be especially useful when you are just beginning to learn about your topic and how it relates to other subjects.

FIGURE C-1: Open Directory Project home page

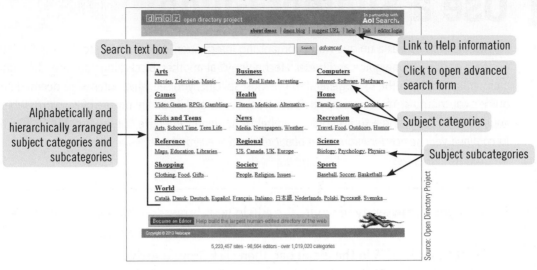

Search text box → □ [Search] *advanced* ← Link to Help information

Click to open advanced search form

Alphabetically and hierarchically arranged subject categories and subcategories

Arts
Movies, Television, Music...

Business
Jobs, Real Estate, Investing...

Computers
Internet, Software, Hardware... ← Subject categories

Games
Video Games, RPGs, Gambling...

Health
Fitness, Medicine, Alternative...

Home
Family, Consumers, Cooking...

Kids and Teens
Arts, School Time, Teen Life...

News
Media, Newspapers, Weather...

Recreation
Travel, Food, Outdoors, Humor...

Reference
Maps, Education, Libraries...

Regional
US, Canada, UK, Europe...

Science
Biology, Psychology, Physics... ← Subject subcategories

Shopping
Clothing, Food, Gifts...

Society
People, Religion, Issues...

Sports
Baseball, Soccer, Basketball...

World
Català, Dansk, Deutsch, Español, Français, Italiano, 日本語, Nederlands, Polski, Русский, Svenska...

Become an Editor Help build the largest human-edited directory of the web

Copyright © 2013 Netscape

5,223,457 sites - 98,564 editors - over 1,019,020 categories

Source: Open Directory Project

FIGURE C-2: Search results for *renewable energy* on the Open Directory Project

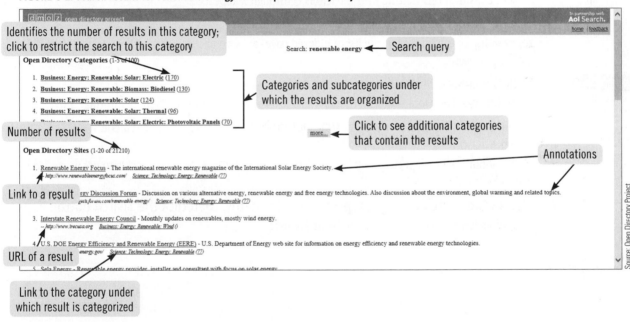

Identifies the number of results in this category; click to restrict the search to this category

Search: **renewable energy** ← Search query

Open Directory Categories (1-5 of 100)

1. Business: Energy: Renewable: Solar: Electric (170)
2. Business: Energy: Renewable: Biomass: Biodiesel (130)
3. Business: Energy: Renewable: Solar (124)
4. Business: Energy: Renewable: Solar: Thermal (96)
5. Business: Energy: Renewable: Solar: Electric: Photovoltaic Panels (70)

Categories and subcategories under which the results are organized

more... ← Click to see additional categories that contain the results

Number of results

Open Directory Sites (1-20 of 21210)

Annotations

1. Renewable Energy Focus - The international renewable energy magazine of the International Solar Energy Society.
   http://www.renewableenergyfocus.com/ Science: Technology: Energy: Renewable (77)

Link to a result rgy Discussion Forum - Discussion on various alternative energy, renewable energy and free energy technologies. Also discussion about the environment, global warming and related topics.
   getsforum.com/renewable energy/ Science: Technology: Energy: Renewable (77)

3. Interstate Renewable Energy Council - Monthly updates on renewables, mostly wind energy.
   http://www.irecusa.org Business: Energy: Renewable: Wind ()

4. U.S. DOE Energy Efficiency and Renewable Energy (EERE) - U.S. Department of Energy web site for information on energy efficiency and renewable energy technologies.
   energy.gov/ Science: Technology: Energy: Renewable (77)

URL of a result

5. Sela Energy - Renewable energy provider, installer and consultant with focus on solar energy.

Link to the category under which result is categorized

Source: Open Directory Project

TABLE C-1: Sampling of subject guides

subject guide	URL	type	features
EERE	eere.energy.gov	Government energy specific	Searchable
INFOMINE	infomine.ucr.edu	Academic/scholarly/distributed	Searchable, created by librarians, high quality
ipl2	ipl2.org	General/reference	Searchable, created by librarians, university-based, high quality
Open Directory Project	dmoz.org	General/distributed	Largest human-edited directory, maintained by volunteer editors from all over the world who need to apply and be accepted as an expert
Scout Archives	scout.wisc.edu/Archives	Academic/reference	Searchable, university-based, high quality
WWW Virtual Library	vlib.org	Academic/general/distributed	First subject guide on the web

©2014 Cengage Learning

Finding Specialty Information

Use a Subject Guide

Each subject guide has a unique way of organizing information. Links relating to "Energy" might appear under "Science" at one guide and under "Technology" at another. By clicking your way through the hierarchy of topics, from the most general to the most specific, you see which sites were deemed best by the guide's contributors. You can also search using keywords, and if you are unsure of keywords when starting your research, browsing a subject guide can help you identify effective ones to use. **CASE** ▶ *You decide to continue your search for information about alternative energy by browsing a few subject guides. You start with the Scout Archives.*

STEPS

1. **Start your browser, type** scout.wisc.edu **in your browser's Address bar, then press [Enter]**
   The site appears, with a menu bar at the top of the home page, and Search text box in the top right corner.

2. **Point to** ARCHIVES **in the menu bar, then click** Browse Archives
   A Browse Resources page opens, with links to classifications (categories) of resources organized alphabetically.

3. **Click the** Q-R link
   A list of classifications starting with the letters *Q* through *R* appears.

4. **Click the** Renewable energy sources link
   Your results appear, and above the list of indexed pages are several classifications or subcategories to further focus your results.

5. **Click the** United States link **under Classification**
   See **FIGURE C-3**. The More Info Link that appears next to each result provides more information.

6. **Scroll down and find a search result that looks interesting, then click the** More Info link **for that result**
   Details about the item appear, similar to those shown in **FIGURE C-4**. Now you decide to use *renewable energy* as keywords for a search.

7. **Click in the** Search text box, **type** renewable energy, **then click the** Search button
   A list of search results appear from the Scout Archives.

Understanding distributed subject guides

WWW Virtual Library and the Open Directory Project are examples of distributed subject guides. Some subject guides are maintained in one location by individuals or organizations. Others, called **distributed subject guides**, are created by a variety of contributors who work somewhat independently on a subtopic of a main topic and are maintained on more than one computer. These guides are said to be "distributed" because rather than being on one computer, the web pages for different parts of the guide are stored on different computers, which are distributed around the country or around the world. Because distributed subject guides have many contributors working independently, each with varying levels of expertise and resources, distributed subject guides tend to have an uneven quality and a lack of standardization. However, this potential downside is balanced by the fact that these different parts of the guide's index are usually maintained by subject experts with a high level of awareness of what is available on the web in their field. Note that in a distributed subject guide, clicking categories might direct your browser to a site on a different web server.

FIGURE C-3: Drill-down results through Renewable energy sources/United States on the Scout Archives

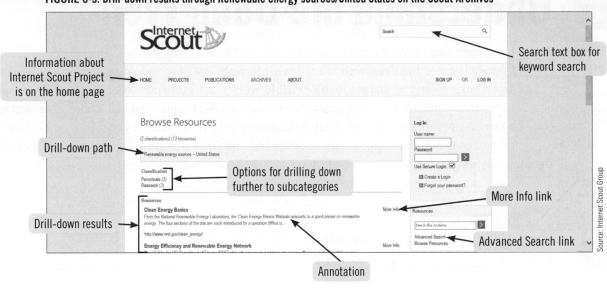

Information about Internet Scout Project is on the home page

Search text box for keyword search

Drill-down path

Options for drilling down further to subcategories

More Info link

Drill-down results

Advanced Search link

Annotation

FIGURE C-4: Details for a search result on the Scout Archives

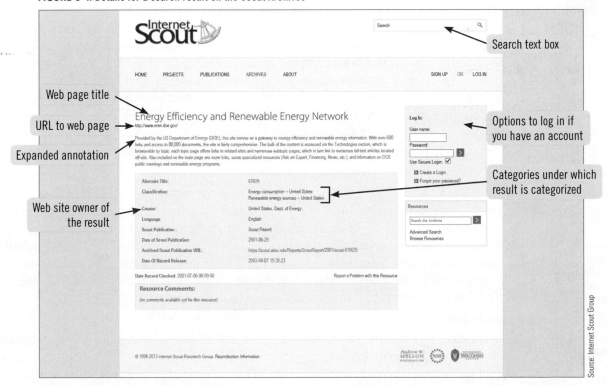

Web page title

Search text box

URL to web page

Options to log in if you have an account

Expanded annotation

Categories under which result is categorized

Web site owner of the result

Internet Research

Understand the Deep Web

Learning
Outcome
• Determine
characteristics
of specialty
search tools

By far, the largest part of the Internet is hidden from most search tools. As you learned in Unit A, this hidden content is called the **deep web** or the **invisible web**. The search engines you have used so far search for information on the **surface web** or **visible web**, which is the portion of the web indexed by traditional search engine spiders. Deep web content largely resides in online databases and is unavailable to traditional search engines because these databases require direct queries at their sites. Common examples are online phone books or newspaper and magazine archives. Other examples include **dynamically generated web pages**, which are web pages that databases create based on specific queries or pages that require a login name and password. FIGURE C-5 provides a conceptual view of Internet content searched by traditional search engines contrasted with the content searched by specialty search tools. **CASE** *Not wanting to ignore a large part of the information available via the Internet, you decide to learn about research tools that can help make the invisible web accessible.*

DETAILS

The following are important considerations when using specialty search tools:

- **Specialty information**

  Typically, you locate hidden web content by going to a specialty web site and using its search form to query a database. Although much of the invisible web is available publicly, some specialized databases require subscriptions. Because libraries pay the subscription fees for many of these specialty sites, they are a good place to access these resources. Some examples of these databases are ProQuest and EBSCOhost. You can also go to a "virtual library" such as the WWW Virtual Library (vlib.org), which links to these specialty web sites from its reference section.

- **Scope and focus**

  By definition, specialty search engines and directories tend to have a narrower and deeper focus, usually resulting in higher-quality content. However, even two tools that focus on the same narrow area are not exactly alike. For example, various governmental agencies are charged with creating access to different, but sometimes overlapping, government information. The National Technical Information Service (NTIS) has a database of government publications on scientific, technical, and business-related topics. The U.S. Census Bureau database primarily focuses on web sites containing demographic information, but also features data related to business and research. The Government Printing Office (GPO) is charged with making much of the information produced by the federal government accessible to citizens. State governments also usually provide their own searchable sites.

- **Cost**

  Most specialty web sites are either free or partially free. If they are commercial sites, they might give away some information but charge you for detailed data. Other sites might allow you free access, but require you to register with them—some require only an email address or username and others require considerably more personal information. Some sites, including many newspaper sites, allow free access to their most recent files but charge for access to archival files. If a site is going to charge you up front, it requires your credit card number, so don't give it out unless you want them to use it.

- **Accessibility**

  Up-to-date, detailed information about people or businesses is hard to come by and, therefore, valuable. Companies guard proprietary information with security measures that prevent unauthorized access. So, although specialty web sites provide access to much of the invisible web, some portions remain hidden.

FIGURE C-5: Internet content searched by traditional search tools contrasted with content searched by specialty search tools*

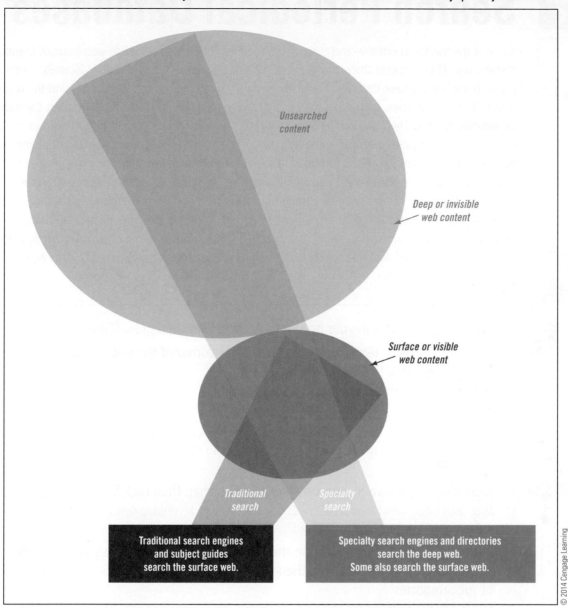

Unsearched content

Deep or invisible web content

Surface or visible web content

Traditional search

Specialty search

Traditional search engines and subject guides search the surface web.

Specialty search engines and directories search the deep web. Some also search the surface web.

© 2014 Cengage Learning

Conceptual only. If this figure were to scale, the deep web portion would be dozens of times larger than the surface web.

Comparing the visible and invisible web

It is impossible to know the exact size of the invisible or deep web; however, a conservative estimate places it at approximately 500 times larger than the visible or surface web. Since the surface web has more than a trillion pages, the deep web is likely more than 500 trillion pages in size. In other words, about 99.8 percent of the information on the web is largely hidden from the view of traditional search engines.

Search Periodical Databases

Some of the most authoritative and current information hidden in the invisible web is stored in **periodical databases**. These include the archives of magazines, newspapers, and scholarly journals. Some sites on the web are "online newsstands." They collect links to electronic periodicals from around the world on all topics. Some periodicals, such as *Salon* or *First Monday*, exist only in electronic format on the web. Other periodicals, such as *The Times* or *The New York Times*, have an online version that might not carry all the same stories as the printed version and might include some stories not seen in print. Most online periodical databases provide limited recent information for free, but require payment for older, archived materials, and some require users to pay for a subscription to access all articles. Some require registration but may ask you to log in only after reading a certain number of articles. Subscription databases such as ProQuest store electronic versions of thousands of periodical titles. **TABLE C-2** describes differences between types of periodicals and gives an example of each type. **CASE** ▶ *Before leaving for the conference in Washington, D.C., you decide to look for some current articles on renewable energy topics to read on the plane. You begin your search with* The Times.

STEPS

TROUBLE
If your search did
not find any articles,
try another search
using another alter-
native energy topic.
If your search still
does not yield any
articles, enter any
other keywords.

1. **Type thetimes.co.uk in your browser's Address Bar, then press [Enter]**

2. **Click in the Search text box in the upper right corner of the page, type renewable energy, then click the Search button**

   Your search results appear, listing links to relevant articles.

3. **Scroll the results page**

   This page sorts results by relevancy, but you notice that you also have the option of sorting by newest or oldest, or refining the search by date. Next, you want to try searching a periodical database that indexes multiple titles.

QUICK TIP
When you use peri-
odical databases, you
might encounter
some articles that are
available to subscrib-
ers only. Your librar-
ian can usually get
these articles for you.

4. **Type magportal.com in your browser's Address bar, then click Search**

   MagPortal offers broad topical categories you can navigate by drilling down to find articles of interest as well as a search engine for keyword searching of the database.

5. **In the list of subject categories in the Search for Magazine Articles list box, click the Science & Technology link, then click the Environment & Geology link in the list of subcategories**

   FIGURE C-6 shows results from drilling down through the subject categories. A Search Articles text box is also available on the results page. The all articles option button is selected by default below the Search Articles text box.

QUICK TIP
Note the annota-
tions, which can help
you quickly identify
which articles might
be most useful.

6. **Click in the Search Articles text box, type renewable energy, then click Search**

   FIGURE C-7 shows the search results page. The small wavy line icon at the end of each article links you to similar articles. You notice that you can sort your results several ways. The results are currently sorted by quality of match, as shown in the order by list box.

FIGURE C-6: MagPortal subject categories results

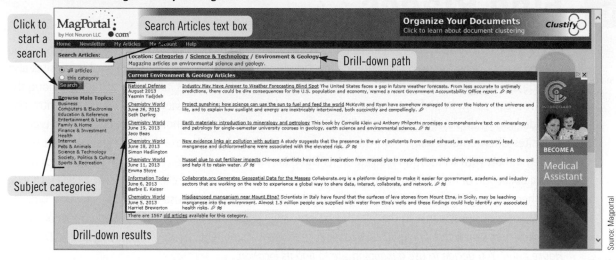

FIGURE C-7: MagPortal search results

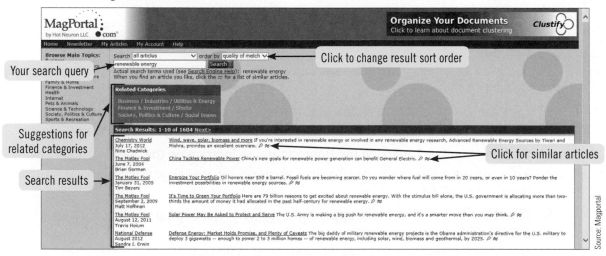

TABLE C-2: Periodicals and their distinguishing characteristics

periodical type	purpose	publisher	audience	documentation	example
Scholarly/ research	Opinions and research in education	University/ organization	Scholars/ professionals/ university students	Citations/ bibliography	*Harvard Educational Review*
Professional/ special interest	Professional practice/ case studies	Organization	Professionals/ university students	May cite or provide bibliography	*Journal of Accountancy*
General interest	Inform/entertain	Commercial	Knowledgeable reader/possibly technical	May mention sources	*The New York Times*
Popular	Entertain	Commercial	General audience/ simple language	Rarely mentions sources	*People Magazine*

Find Places

Learning
Outcome
• Search a mapping
  site to get
  directions

Before the World Wide Web, you had to buy a map or call for directions to find out how to get where you wanted to go. Now the web offers quite a few good map and locator web sites. Many of these sites also provide trip planners, driving directions, and links to hotels, historical sites, and other attractions along the way. You can zoom in and out of maps to see more detail or a broader view of the area. Many sites also provide links to display the map in satellite view or a view that displays photos of the area. Other types of web sites often embed maps from these sites on their own pages; for example, a hotel web site might embed a map with its location marked on its Directions or Location page. The Library of Congress maintains a collection of historical maps that you can view by going to loc.gov, clicking DIGITAL COLLECTIONS, and then clicking Map Collections. **TABLE C-3** lists several map sites. To use a mapping site, you type an address or a business name in the Search text box. **CASE** *You plan to attend a Department of Energy Efficiency and Renewable Energy (EERE) conference in Washington, D.C. You will be staying at the Donovan House hotel. You decide to use a mapping site to find its location.*

STEPS

1. **Type** mapquest.com **in your browser's Address bar, then press [Enter]**
    The MapQuest home page opens. It might show a map of the entire United States, your local area, or another local area.

2. **Click in the SEARCH FOR text box, type** Donovan House, Washington, DC, **then click Get Map**
    A map of the Washington, D.C., area appears with the Donovan House identified on the map. See **FIGURE C-8**.

3. **Click the Zoom In button on the map three times**
    The map zooms in so you can clearly see that the Donovan House is located on 14th Street Northwest.

4. **Click the number 1 marking the Donovan House location on the map**
    A pop-up window opens giving the full address, phone number, and links to more information for Donovan House. See **FIGURE C-9**.

5. **Click the Close button in the upper-right corner of the pop-up window, then click SATELLITE in the upper-right corner of the map**
    The view from a satellite appears with the map overlaid on the image.

6. **Click LIVE TRAFFIC in the upper-right corner of the map**
    You see colored lines appear on the map that overlays the satellite image. Green indicates that traffic is flowing at a normal pace, yellow indicates that there is moderately heavy traffic and it is moving a little slower than normal, and red indicates that traffic is very heavy and is moving very slowly.

FIGURE C-8: Map of Washington, D.C., area with Donovan House identified

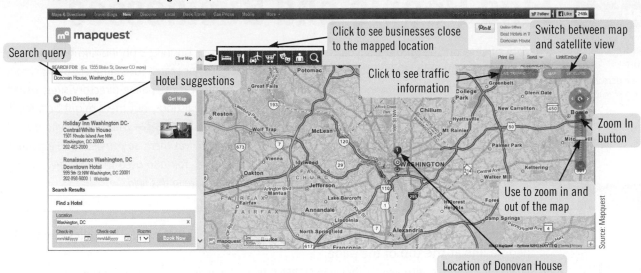

Search query

Hotel suggestions

Click to see businesses close to the mapped location

Switch between map and satellite view

Click to see traffic information

Zoom In button

Use to zoom in and out of the map

Location of Donovan House

Source: Mapquest

FIGURE C-9: Details for Donovan House hotel

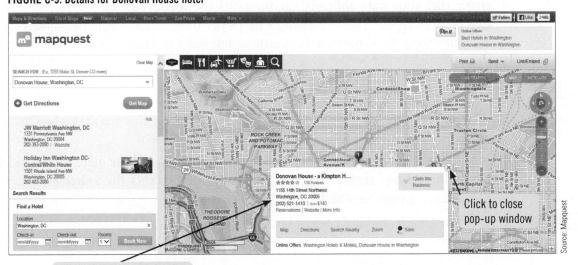

Click to close pop-up window

Window showing hotel details

Source: Mapquest

TABLE C-3: Mapping web sites

web site	URL	features
Google Maps	maps.google.com	Traffic updates, satellite view, street photos, walking directions, public transit directions, bicycling directions
Bing Maps	bing.com/maps	Traffic updates, satellite view, photos from the air, street photos, walking directions, public transit information
MapQuest	mapquest.com	Traffic updates, satellite view, country-specific mapping sites including the United Kingdom (mapquest.co.uk), Germany (mapquest.de), and France (mapquest.fr)
Streetmap	streetmap.co.uk	Lists businesses in the area
Rand McNally Travel Store	maps.randmcnally.com	Lists businesses in the area, videos of sites in area
Yahoo! Maps	maps.yahoo.com	Traffic updates, satellite view

©2014 Cengage Learning

Internet Research

Find People and Businesses

Learning Outcomes
• Locate a person
• Locate a business

A variety of sites on the web allow you to search for a person's or business's phone number and street address just as you would search the white pages of a phone book, or search for a business using categories just like a printed yellow pages directory. **TABLE C-4** lists some of these online directory sites. Usually, there is no charge to a business for the basic address and telephone listings, but there might be a fee if a business wants to include a link to its web site or an advertisement. **CASE** *When you attend the EERE conference in Washington, D.C., you hope to meet with a relative who lives there, so you decide to experiment with an online directory so that you can use one to find your relative. You also need to find experts in wind energy, so you will search for businesses and organizations that specialize in this field.*

STEPS

1. **Type** yellowpages.com **in your browser's Address bar, press [Enter], then click the** Find People link **at the top of the page**

   The People Search page opens, as shown in **FIGURE C-10**. First, you want to look for someone in your city or town who shares your name.

2. **Click in the** First Name text box, **type your first initial, click in the** Last Name text box, **type your last name, click in the** City or ZIP Code text box, **type your city, click the** State arrow, **click your state abbreviation, then click the** Search button

   A list of names appears. Directory searches often provide better results using just an initial, rather than a first name. Notice the Map and Driving Directions links under each result. Most directories that list white and yellow pages results include links to a mapping site, allowing you to jump instantly to a map of the location where the person or business is located.

3. **Click your name or another name in the list or results**

   A new page opens with data for the person whose name you clicked. Now you want to find businesses and organizations in the field of wind energy in the Washington, D.C., area.

4. **Click in the** What are you looking for? text box **at the top of the page, type** wind energy, **click in the** Where? text box, **type** Washington DC, **then click the** Search button

   A list of results appears. See **FIGURE C-11**.

5. **Click the** American Wind Energy Association link

   Details about the American Wind Energy Association appear, including the address, phone number, a link to their web site, and a map of their location.

Finding personal email addresses and telephone numbers

Some white pages sites search for email addresses, but, largely due to spamming, most people no longer want their email addresses available to spiders on the web. Also, email addresses tend to change frequently, even for professional or commercial sites, so addresses found through searches might be out of date. Telephone numbers can also be difficult to find for those who have opted out of being listed in telephone directories.

FIGURE C-10: People Search page on Yellowpages.com

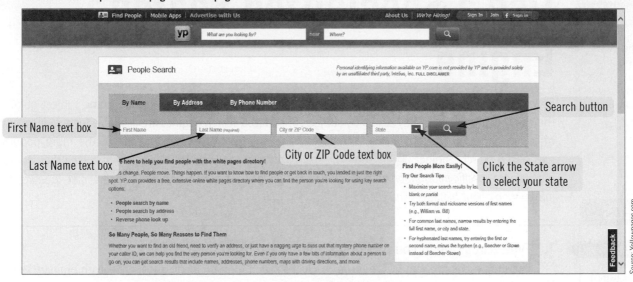

First Name text box

Last Name text box

Search button

City or ZIP Code text box

Click the State arrow to select your state

FIGURE C-11: Results for *wind energy* in Washington, D.C. on Yellowpages.com

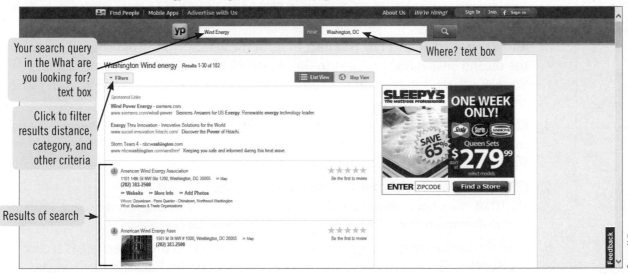

Your search query in the What are you looking for? text box

Where? text box

Click to filter results distance, category, and other criteria

Results of search

TABLE C-4: Features of selected business finder web sites

web site	country	white pages	yellow pages	maps
AnyWho.com	US	X	X	X
Canada411.ca	Canada	X	X	
Europages.com	Europe	X		
Scoot.co.uk	UK	X	X	X
Superpages.com	US	X	X	X
UKphonebook.com	UK	X	X	X
Whitepages.com	US	X		
Yell.com	UK		X	
Yellowpages.com	US	X	X	X
Yellowpages.ca	Canada	X	X	X
Yellowpages.com.au	Australia	X	X	X

Use a Specialized Search Engine

Specialized search engines are similar to regular web search engines, except, like some subject guides, they limit the web pages they search by subject. Specialized search engines are available for a wide variety of topics, including law, medicine, computers, and energy. **TABLE C-5** lists some of the more popular specialized search engines. **CASE** *The specialized search engine Scirus is a search engine that indexes only science-specific information on the Internet. You decide to use this specialized search engine to search for information about biomass wind energy.*

STEPS

1. **Type scirus.com in your browser's Address bar, then press [Enter]**

   The site's home page appears. You can conduct a search from the home page, or, as with ordinary search engines, you can use the site's Advanced search page.

2. **Click the Advanced search link**

   The Advanced search page appears, as shown in **FIGURE C-12**. Notice that All of the words and the Boolean operator AND are the default selections for creating a search phrase.

3. **Click in the first Search text box next to All of the words, type "wind energy", click in the second Search text box next to the second All of the words, then type biomass**

   Now you will specify that only recent results should be returned. The default is to return results published before 1900 through the current year.

4. **Click the before 1900 list arrow in the Dates section, then click the year two years prior to the current year**

   You only want to see results that are web pages.

5. **Click the HTML check box in the File formats section**

   The HTML check box is selected and the Any format check box is automatically deselected. Finally, you want to show results only in the Engineering, Energy and Technology category.

6. **Click the Engineering, Energy and Technology check box in the Subject areas section**

   The check box you clicked is selected and the All subject areas check box is automatically deselected.

7. **Click Search**

   Web pages from scientific sources or about scientific topics that include your search phrase appear.

FIGURE C-12: Scirus Advanced search page

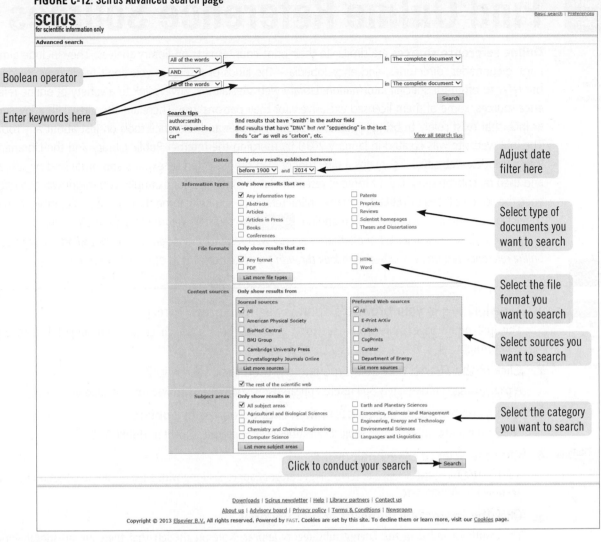

TABLE C-5: Specialized Search Engines

specialized search engine	description
Scirus.com	Offers an advanced search form for finding information using a comprehensive science-specific search engine that indexes over 575 million science-specific web pages.
MedlinePlus.com	Lets you search for information about diseases and health and wellness issues, providing results that most people can easily comprehend. Sponsored by the National Institutes of Health and produced by the U.S. National Library of Medicine.
iSEEK.com	Targeted search engine with an extensive collection of authoritative resources from university, government, and respected noncommercial providers.
FindLaw.com	Offers the largest free legal search engine for finding information about legal cases in specified courts, contracts, and legal articles categorized by topics such as law technology, law practice, and legal news.
Business.com	Comprehensive business-oriented search engine and subject directory dedicated to all things business. It includes commercial listings, along with noncommercial results based on editorial criteria.

Internet Research

Find Online Reference Sources

Learning Outcome
• Research online reference sources

Online reference sources are similar to their print counterparts on library shelves. They include almanacs, dictionaries, directories, and encyclopedias—the kinds of resources you don't read cover to cover, but refer to often for specific information. Library web sites almost always link to a variety of online reference sources, some of them licensed exclusively for their patrons' use. There are also virtual libraries, such as ipl2, that exist solely to bring together valuable web sites and reference tools on just about any topic. The ipl2 web site was created in January 2010 by merging the Internet Public Library and the Librarians' Internet Index web sites. It contains a directory of web sites selected by experts and organized by subject and then by subcategory. If your topic of research was the Internet, for example, you might want to reference the sources listed in **TABLE C-6**. Many online reference sources can be thought of as a combination of subject guide and a specialized search engine. **CASE** *You have returned from the EERE conference and are ready to finish your final list of alternative energy web resources, but you would like to find a few reliable online reference resources. You decide to look through the reference sources at the ipl2 web site.*

STEPS

QUICK TIP
When you find good reference sites, add them to your browser's Favorites or Bookmarks file for easy access.

1. **Type ipl2.org in your browser's Address bar, then press [Enter]**
   The ipl2 home page appears. You see that ipl2 offers both a search engine and subject headings to drill through.

2. **Click in the Search text box, type energy, then click Search ipl2**
   A page listing approximately 500 results appears. Now you want to browse the resources by subject.

3. **Click your browser's Back button, then click Resources by Subject**
   The Resources by Subject main subject categories page appears as shown in **FIGURE C-13**.

TROUBLE
If nothing appears and if you are using Internet Explorer, click the Compatibility View button in the Address bar.

4. **Click the Science & Technology link**
   A list of results in the Science & Technology category appears, along with a list of subcategories on the left, as shown in **FIGURE C-14**.

5. **Click the Energy link in the list of subcategories**
   The results included in the Energy subcategory appear. Note on the left that there are no subcategories within the Energy subcategory. You want to try a different online reference source.

6. **Type infoplease.com in your browser's Address bar, then press [Enter]**
   The Infoplease home page appears.

7. **Point to the Science & Health link in the menu bar at the top of the page**
   A list of subcategories in the Science & Health category appears.

8. **Click the Environment & Energy link to display the Environment and Nature page, then click the Energy link**
   The list of resources in the Energy subcategory appears.

9. **Click the Renewable Energy Consumption in the U.S. by Source, 1989–2010 link**
   A table appears, showing how much renewable energy was used in the United States from 1989 to 2010.

FIGURE C-13: Subject headings on ipl2

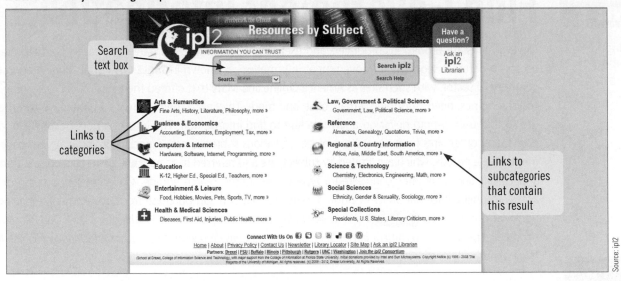

FIGURE C-14: Results in the Science and Technology category with subcategories on ipl2

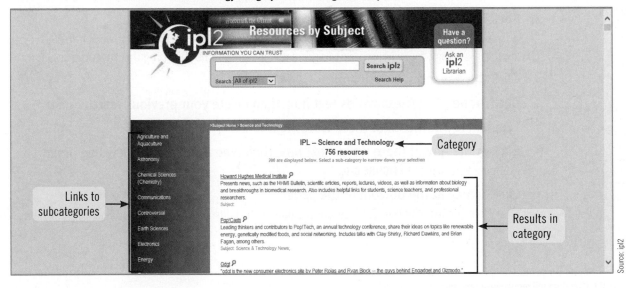

TABLE C-6: Resources for information on "the Internet" topic

name	URL	features
ipl2	ipl2.org	Provides reliable links to answer almost any Internet question; covers searching, web design, history, law, children, and more
FILExt	filext.com	Lists most Internet file extensions; defines extensions and links to more information
Netiquette Home Page	albion.com/netiquette	Provides the basics of Netiquette, at work and at home; covers primarily online communication
Webopedia	webopedia.com	Covers computer and Internet terminology; provides paragraph encyclopedia definitions and links
Living Internet	livinginternet.com	Covers the Internet, the web, email, chat, newsgroups, and mailing lists; articles include history and how-to information

**Internet Research
UNIT C**

**Learning
Outcome**
• Search govern-
ment portals

Find Government Information

Governments are prodigious producers and users of information. Large gateways, called **portals**, create access to different segments of government information, as shown in **TABLE C-7**. Portals originated in the commercial sector, with such sites as America Online and MSN that offered their version of "everything"—search engines, news, shopping, email, chat, and more. They each tried to create an attractive and useful site so that users would never go anywhere else to find information. The idea of a portal caught on, and now many other sites have carved out niches in various subject areas, especially in industry and government. These portals, which are limited by subject, are also referred to as **vortals**, or vertical portals. Portals and vortals are sometimes considered a type of specialized search engine. Government portals provide access to online information or to printed materials that you can purchase from government agencies or borrow from libraries. **CASE** ▶ *While attending the EERE conference in Washington, D.C., you heard of a good place to access government information online—USA.gov. You want to see what information you can find there about wind energy and other alternative energy resources.*

STEPS

1. **Type usa.gov in your browser's Address bar, then press [Enter]**
   The USA.gov web site opens. You can use either the Search text box or point to Topics to display a list of topics you can use to drill down through subject headings.

2. **Click in the Search text box, type wind energy, then click SEARCH**
   A list of search results opens, as shown in **FIGURE C-15**. You want to expand your search to find results for alternative energy, renewable energy, or green energy. You can do this using the Advanced Search form.

3. **Click the Advanced Search link**

4. **Click in the All of these words text box, then delete your previous search query**

5. **Type energy in the All of these words text box**

6. **Click in the Any of these words text box, then type alternative renewable green**
   Compare your screen to **FIGURE C-16**.

7. **Click Search at the bottom of the page**
   The web pages listed in the search results include the text *alternative energy, renewable energy,* or *green energy.*

TABLE C-7: Specialized government portals

name	URL	features
GOV.UK	www.gov.uk	Central and local government information for the United Kingdom
FedWorld	fedworld.ntis.gov	Sponsored by the National Technical Information Service (NTIS); includes scientific, technical, business, and engineering information; contains links to reports and publications available for purchase
Government of Canada	canada.gc.ca	Canadian federal, provincial, and municipal information
GPO(Government Printing Office)	www.gpo.gov/fdsys	Contains links to federal publications; provides catalog of government documents available for purchase; contains a catalog of libraries that own specific documents
University of Michigan Government Documents Center	lib.umich.edu/clark-library	Most complete guide to government information; contains links to local, state, national, and international government sites
USA.gov	usa.gov	Most comprehensive site for U.S. government information and services; contains links to over 20,000 federal and state government web sites

FIGURE C-15: Search results for *wind energy* on USA.gov

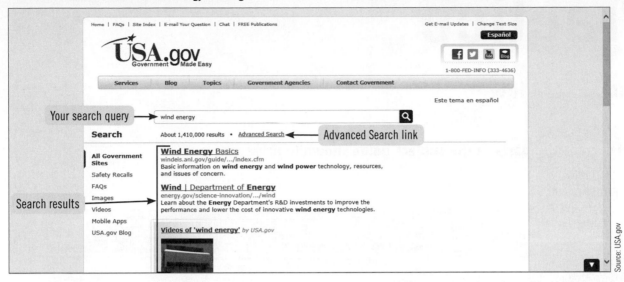

FIGURE C-16: Advanced Search page on USA.gov

Finding state and provincial government sites

You might want to use government sites to locate web sites for U.S. states or Canadian provinces. A search with *government* and the name of the state or province usually finds the official home page in the first few results. In addition, there are sites that contain pages that are portals to the official home pages of state and provincial government web sites.

Practice

Concepts Review

Label each of the parts in the subject guide shown in FIGURE C-17.

FIGURE C-17

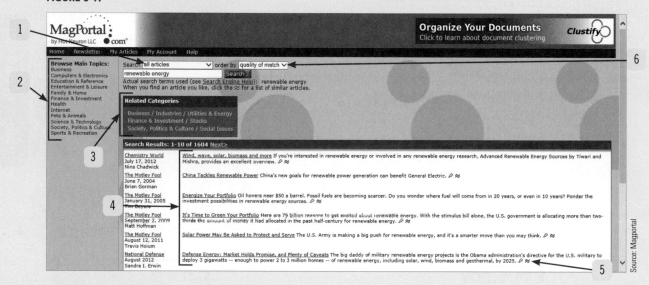

Source: Magportal

Match each term with the statement that best describes it.

7. **Invisible web** i
8. **Subject guide** d
9. **Online reference sources** a
10. **Portal** b
11. **ipl2** g
12. **Drill down** f
13. **Specialized search engine** h
14. **Dynamically generated web page** e
15. **Visible web** c

a. Similar to print counterparts on library shelves
b. A gateway to large segments of related web information
c. The portion of the web accessible to traditional search engines and directories
d. Indexed web pages maintained by experts and organized into hierarchical and alphabetical topics
e. A web page that is generated when you request it
f. To browse or click through a hierarchy of topics and subtopics to reach links on a results page
g. An example of a virtual library
h. A search engine that limits the web pages it searches by subject
i. The portion of the web not accessible to traditional search engines

Select the best answer from the list of choices.

16. **Specialty search tools might** ___d___ .
    a. give away some information but charge for some too
    b. require you to pay for the service
    c. allow you a few free searches and ask you to pay for more
    d. all of the above

17. **The invisible web** ___c___ .
    a. is much smaller than the visible web
    b. consists mostly of dynamically generated web pages
    c. is also known as the deep web
    d. is not accessible

18. **Which of the following are traits that all subject guides share?** d
    a. They are organized hierarchically and are selective in the web sites they list.
    b. They are relatively small compared with search engines.
    c. They include annotations to the web sites they index.
    d. All of the above.

19. **A good place to search for information about businesses in the United Kingdom is** ___b___ .
    a. ipl2
    b. Scoot
    c. Switchboard
    d. Yellowpages.ca

20. **A site with links to local, state, national, and international governments is** ___c___ .
    a. FirstGov
    b. United States Government Printing Office
    c. FedWorld
    d. University of Michigan Documents Center

21. **One definition of browsing is** ___c___ .
    a. using a local search engine to search a subject guide
    b. using criteria to evaluate a web site
    c. clicking through the hierarchy of topics at a subject guide
    d. finding out who wrote a web page

22. **Which of the following is not an example of an online reference source?** c
    a. Almanacs
    b. Encyclopedias
    c. Metasearch engine
    d. Dictionaries

23. **A distributed subject guide** ___d___ .
    a. is maintained by one editor
    b. is the same thing as a search engine
    c. usually resides on one computer
    d. might lack standardization

Skills Review

If requested by your instructor, create a document listing the answers to the questions asked in the following exercises.

1. Understand subject guides.

  a. Describe how subject guides are organized.

  b. Explain how subject guides limit the web pages they index.

  c. Describe the two ways you can find a list of results in a subject guide.

  d. Explain why annotations help users determine which results are relevant.

  e. Explain why the results from a subject guide can be more useful than the results from a search engine.

2. Use a subject guide.

  a. Start your browser, then go to the Open Directory Project at **dmoz.org**.

  b. To find information about environmental health education, drill down to the results under the following path: Science/Environment/Environmental Health/Education. Note the path at the top of the page. If requested by your instructor, print or save this page of results.

  c. Return to the Open Directory Project home page, then display the subcategories in the Health category. Note the path at the top of the page.

  d. Display the subcategories in the Environmental Health subcategory. Note the path at the top of the page. Why do you think the path changed?

  e. Display the results in the Education subcategory. Note the number of results after the path, and then examine the results and the annotations.

  f. Use the Search text box at the top of the page to conduct a search of the entire directory using the keywords *"environmental health" education*. Note the number of results. If requested by your instructor, print or save this page of results.

  g. Scroll down and examine the paths under each result. Are they the same or different as the drill-down path?

  h. Examine the list of results, identify the result that seems like it is the most relevant, and then follow that link to see if the web page provides you with the information you want. If requested by your instructor, print or save this page.

3. Understand the deep web.

  a. Explain what the invisible web is.

  b. Explain what the visible web is.

  c. Describe dynamically generated web pages.

  d. Explain why results from specialty search engines and directories are higher-quality content than results from ordinary search engines.

4. Search periodical databases.

  a. Go to **magportal.com**.

  b. Drill down through the Education & Reference/Technology in Education categories. Click a subcategory that interests you. If requested by your instructor, print or save this page of results.

  c. Follow a link to one of the results. Read the article. (Note that you can click the "old articles" link to list articles that are older than a month or so.) If requested by your instructor, print or save this page.

  d. Click your browser's Back button, use the Search Articles text box to create a search query based on the article you just read, type the search query in the Search text box, and then conduct your search. If requested by your instructor, print or save this page of results.

    e. Examine your results, and then click a few links and scan the articles. Are they about the topic for which you searched? If not, rephrase your search query, and try your search again.

    f. Go to **nytimes.com**.

    g. Search for an article on this site using the same search query. If requested by your instructor, print or save this page of results.

    h. Examine the results. Are the stories about the right topic?

5. Find places.

    a. Go to **mapquest.com**.

    b. Find the location of the Union Oyster House restaurant in Boston, Massachusetts.

    c. Zoom in until you can see the name of the street the restaurant is on. If requested by your instructor, print or save this page.

    d. Switch to Satellite view, and then zoom in until the image changes from a satellite image to a photo taken from the sky. (The details in the image will become clearer.)

    e. Display the traffic conditions.

    f. Go to **maps.google.com**, and then find the same restaurant. If requested by your instructor, print or save this page.

6. Find people and businesses.

    a. Go to **411locate.com**.

    b. Use the Locate a Person form to search for yours or a friend's information. If requested by your instructor, print or save this page of results.

    c. Click the view details link below yours or your friend's name on the results page. If there are no results, try a different name.

    d. Return to the home page on 411 Locate, and then use the Reverse Phone Lookup form to run a search on your home phone number. If requested by your instructor, print or save this page of results.

    e. Return to the Reverse Phone Lookup form on 411 Locate, and then use the Lookup form to search for your cell phone number. If requested by your instructor, print or save this page of results.

    f. Go to **switchboard.com**.

    g. Think of a business in your city or town, type its business category (such as accountants, newspapers, schools, or veterinarians) or business name, and type your city and state, and then click Find. (If there are no resulting businesses, go back and enter another type of business.) If requested by your instructor, print or save this page of results.

    h. Scroll down the results page. Is the business you thought of listed?

7. Use a specialized search engine.

    a. Go to **envirolink.org**. This is a specialized search engine for environmental web sites.

    b. Use the Search text box to search for **green energy**. Note the number of results. If requested by your instructor, print or save this page of results.

    c. Return to the home page, and then view the subcategories in the Energy category. Note the number of results in each of the following subcategories (as indicated by the number in parentheses after the subcategory name): Biomass, Geothermal Energy, Solar Energy, and Wind Energy. If requested by your instructor, print or save this page of results.

    d. Examine the results in the Wind Energy subcategory. If requested by your instructor, print or save this page of results.

    e. Click one of the results to examine the information presented on that site.

Skills Review (continued)

8. **Find online reference sources.**

   a. Go to **ipl2.org**.

   b. Click Special Collections Created by ipl2, and then click the A+ Research/Writing Guide button. If requested by your instructor, print or save this page.

   c. Click the Table of Contents link, and then explore the resource.

   d. Return to the ipl2 home page, click Resources by Subject, click the Reference link, and then click the Style and Writing Guides subcategory link. If requested by your instructor, print or save this page of results.

   e. Scroll down and click the Purdue University Online Writing Lab (OWL) link. Click the link on the OWL site that leads you to information on the APA formatting and style guidelines. Read this information. If requested by your instructor, print or save this page.

   f. Return to the Purdue Online Writing Lab (OWL) home page, and then click the link that leads you to information on the MLA formatting and style guidelines. Read this information. If requested by your instructor, print or save this page.

9. **Find government information.**

   a. Go to **usa.gov**.

   b. Conduct a search using the search query **senator**. Examine the wide range of results. If requested by your instructor, print or save this page of results.

   c. Click the Advanced Search link.

   d. Make sure *senator* is in the All of these words text box.

   e. Click in the This exact phrase text box, and then type **committee chair**.

   f. Click Search at the bottom of the page. How did this narrow the search results? If requested by your instructor, print or save this page of results.

Independent Challenge 1

You want to start exporting the products your business sells to Canada and Australia. You want to do some research to find information on each country's regulations.

   a. Go to the web site for the Canadian government at **canada.gc.ca**, and click English to access the English version of the web site.

   b. Conduct a search using the search query **importing goods**. Examine the results. If requested by your instructor, print or save this page of results.

   c. Click the Advanced Search link and use it to narrow the search to regulations for importing goods to Canada. If requested by your instructor, print or save this page of results. Examine the results again, click one that seems the most likely to contain the answers to your questions, and read the page that opens.

   d. Go to the web site for the Australian government at **australia.gov.au**.

   e. Conduct a search on this site using the same search query as in step b. If requested by your instructor, print or save this page of results.

   f. Examine the results, click one that seems the most likely to contain the answers to your questions, and read the page that opens.

Independent Challenge 2

You have a friend who was just diagnosed with Chronic Fatigue Syndrome and want to learn more about this disease. You decide to use a specialty search engine for finding information about this medical topic.

a. Go to MedlinePlus at **www.nlm.nih.gov/medlineplus**.

b. Search for information about Chronic Fatigue Syndrome. Look over the search results, and if requested by your instructor, print or save this page of results.

c. Notice the Refine by Type and Refine by Keyword filtering boxes along the left side of page. The Refine by Keyword box lets you cluster your search results into groups based on the keywords listed in this box. A plus sign (+) in front of a keyword indicates there are subcategories available for that keyword cluster. You want to learn what drugs and supplements are available to treat your friend's disease.

d. To narrow your search, click the plus sign (+) in front of the Drugs and Supplements keyword in the Refine by Keyword box, then click the Vitamin subcategory. Note the number to the right of each cluster indicates how many search results are available. If requested by your instructor, print or save this page of results.

e. Click several of the search results and scan them for relevant information.

Independent Challenge 3

The first step in getting a job interview in today's highly competitive job market is to create a top-notch résumé. Subject guides can provide invaluable resources to help you prepare the best possible résumé. Because ipl2 is one of the most comprehensive hand-crafted subject guides on the web, you decide to consult it for help with your résumé.

a. Go to **ipl2.org**.

b. Display resources by subject, and then drill down to find the Employment subcategory in the Business and Economics category. If requested by your instructor, print or save this page of results.

c. Click one of the resources listed that offers advice or samples of résumé and cover letters. Explore the suggestions and examples of how to prepare a résumé.

d. Return to the ipl2 home page, and use the Search text box to find results for the search query **resume**. Examine the results. If requested by your instructor, print or save this page of results.

Independent Challenge 4: Explore

You and a business associate are driving in Great Britain from London to Manchester to visit some clients. As you haven't driven there before, you want to get driving directions.

a. Go to the British MapQuest web site at **mapquest.co.uk**.

b. Find the section for directions.

c. Enter the appropriate to and from locations and get the directions. (Note that because the web site identifies the location of your computer, you might need to type **England** after each city name.)

d. On the resulting directions page, locate the Print link, and then click the link.

e. Type your name in the Notes section, deselect the Map check box, deselect the Advertisement check box, and then print the directions.

f. Go to the North American MapQuest web site at **mapquest.com**.

g. Click the link to get driving directions. Find the driving distance between Quebec, QC, and Vancouver, BC. Note the total distance. If requested by your instructor, print or save this page.

h. Click the Options link, and then select the option to calculate the directions so that the driving occurs all within Canada and not within the United States. (*Hint*: Select the appropriate checkbox in the Avoid the following section.) Is the total driving distance longer or shorter than your first search? If requested by your instructor, print or save this page.

Visual Workshop

Find the web page shown in **FIGURE C-18**. To start, go the home page of the Open Directory project (**dmoz.org**). After you find the page, click one of the results.

FIGURE C-18

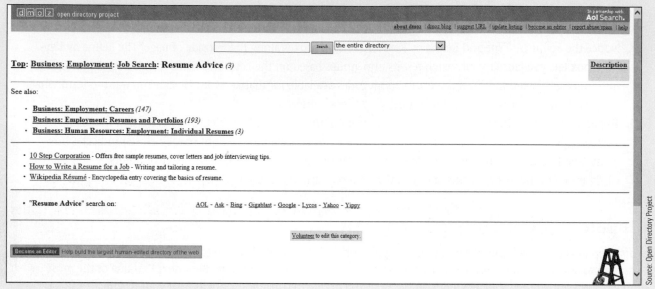

Searching the Social Web

CASE At a conference in Washington, D.C., on renewable energy, you met several specialists in windmill turbines and biomass as renewable energy sources. Bob Johnson, the reference librarian, suggests that you use the social web to discover additional authorities and information on the subject.

Unit Objectives

After completing this unit, you will be able to:

- Understand social media platforms
- Search social networks
- Navigate the blogosphere
- Scan microblogs
- Search video and photo sharing sites
- Search social news sites
- Find answers with Q&A sites
- Use social media search engines

Files You Will Need

No files needed.

Understand Social Media Platforms

A wide variety of social media platforms exist and each provides a different way for participants to connect with each other. There are over a billion social media participants who collaborate to produce an almost endless stream of content that is hosted on over a billion **social media sites**, which are collectively referred to as the **social web**. Because the content on the social web is generated and organized in large part by people without web design skills, the benefits of **search engine optimization**—the process of fine-tuning a web site so that it ranks at the top of search engine results—are not as prevalent. Instead, users typically provide ad hoc keywords (called **tags**) that help identify the content on the social web. **TABLE D-1** lists popular social media sites and ranks them in order of number of visitors per month. **CASE** *Before searching the social web for information on alternative energy, you decide to familiarize yourself with the major types of social media platforms.*

DETAILS

The following are common categories of social media platforms:

• **Social networks**

  Social networks are online communities where people form relationships based on everything from friendship and workplace affiliations to common interests and shared beliefs. To facilitate this, these sites typically encourage users to create profiles about themselves. Popular social networks include Facebook, Google+, and LinkedIn.

• **Blogs**

  A **blog** (short for **web log**) is regularly published content, such as commentaries, opinions, and announcements, in the form of text, images, and video. Most blogs are interactive, encouraging readers to submit comments, which bloggers sometimes respond to. Blogs and comments are often simply called **posts** or **postings**.

• **Microblogs**

  A **microblog** is a blog that significantly limits the length of posts. Most microblog posts consist of short sentences and links. Twitter, with over 500 million users, is the leading microblogging site. Twitter restricts posts, called **tweets**, to 140 characters. People who send tweets on Twitter are called **Twitterers** and they often include links to sites with more detailed information within their tweets.

• **Video and photo sharing sites**

  People upload and share video clips and images using **video** and **photo sharing sites**. Typically, videos and photos can be shared with the public or restricted for private viewings. YouTube is far and away the most-visited video sharing site, while Pinterest has quickly become the most-visited photo sharing site.

• **Social news sites and social bookmarking sites**

  Social news sites enable users to submit news stories or other web pages and vote on news stories posted by others. The most popular content appears on the coveted front pages of these sites, as illustrated in **FIGURE D-1**. **Social bookmarking sites**, such as Delicious and BlinkList, let people store and describe their favorite web pages with tags, allowing other users to search for popular content.

• **Q&A sites and Wiki sites**

  Q&A (Question and Answer) sites allow people to pose a question and receive answers back from anyone willing and (it is hoped) knowledgeable enough to reply. Quora (founded by two former top Facebook executives) dominates the Q&A site landscape, with over 1.5 million unique monthly visitors. A **wiki** is server software that lets anyone create and modify web page content. A wiki (Hawaiian for *quick*) makes it easy to build and interlink web pages, encouraging group participation in building web content.

FIGURE D-1: Home page on reddit.com

Categories of articles available

Sponsored link

Articles in the Hot category

Click to join the site as an author

Number of viewer comments

You can search for articles

Source: reddit.com

TABLE D-1: Popular social media sites

social media site	type	monthly visitors* (millions)	social media site	type	monthly visitors* (millions)
Facebook facebook.com	Social network	750	Photobucket photobucket.com	Photo sharing site	75.5
YouTube youtube.com	Video sharing site	450	MySpace myspace.com	Social network	75.5
Wikipedia wikipedia.org	Wiki	350	Blogger blogger.com	Blog hosting site	75
Twitter twitter.com	Microblogging site	250	Google+ plus.google.com	Social network	65
WordPress wordpress.com	Blog hosting site	140	Tumblr tumblr.com	Blog hosting site	60
LinkedIn linkedin.com	Social network	110	DailyMotion dailymotion.com	Video sharing site	27
Flickr flickr.com	Photo sharing site	90	reddit reddit.com	Social news site	16
Pinterest pinterest.com	Photo sharing site	85.5	Digg digg.com	Social news site	4.1

*Estimated unique monthly visitors according to eBiz|MBA Knowledgebase, August 2013

©2014 Cengage Learning

Searching the Social Web

Search Social Networks

Social networks, such as Facebook, Google+, and LinkedIn, enable people to easily establish relationships and virtual communities by sharing personal profiles, participating in discussion groups, and exchanging private and public messages. Facebook is the dominant social network with over a billion users from a wide range of ages and walks of life. Google+ is a newer social network, which has rapidly expanded to over a half-billion users. LinkedIn is the fastest growing professional social network, making it a great resource for locating expertise in a variety of fields. Since LinkedIn has a highly structured format, you can find people and businesses with simple keyword searches. For example, if you want to find only people currently working for a particular company, you can enter the name of the company and specify that they are current employees of the organization. **CASE** ▶ *During the renewable energy conference in Washington, D.C., you attended a session on wind energy. You want to find people who have expertise in this specific area of renewable energy. You decide to use LinkedIn to locate these people.*

STEPS

1. **Start your browser, type** linkedin.com **in the Address bar, then press [Enter]**

   The home page for the social network LinkedIn appears in your browser. Although you can search for members on LinkedIn, to take advantage of its full search capabilities and gain access to the details of the current members, you need to be a member yourself.

2. **If you are a LinkedIn member, type your email address in the** Email address text box **and your password in the** Password text box, **then press [Enter]; if you are not a LinkedIn member, use the** Get Started form **to enter your first and last names, email address, and a password, click** Join Now, **then follow the instructions to fill in the necessary information to create a profile**

   After you log in to LinkedIn, you will see your home page. There is a menu bar across the top.

3. **Point to** Profile **in the menu bar, then click** Edit Profile

   A page similar to the one shown in **FIGURE D-2** appears. Each member of LinkedIn provides information about his or her work experience and other relevant information to be displayed on their Profile page. You can search the LinkedIn network by entering a search query in the Search for people, jobs, companies and more text box above the menu bar, or you can use the Advanced search form to take advantage of the LinkedIn search capabilities.

4. **Click the** Advanced link **to the right of the Search for people, jobs, companies and more text box**

   The LinkedIn Advanced People Search form appears, as shown in **FIGURE D-3**. You want to search for people who have expertise in wind energy, and who currently work in the renewable energy industry.

5. **Click in the** Keywords text box, **type** wind energy, **click the** Industry link, **scroll down the list and click the** Renewables & Environment check box, **then click** Search

   A list of people appears, as shown in **FIGURE D-4**, and for each you see a job title, location, industry, and current and past work experiences.

6. **Scroll down and examine the search results, then click a link to examine a profile for someone experienced in wind energy**

   If this were a real-world situation, you would click the Connect button to contact this person via email.

Finding discussion groups

A **discussion group** (also called **discussion forums**) provides the means for people to conduct conversations online by exchanging messages asynchronously. Within a discussion group, topics are further broken into subtopics called **threads**, which arrange messages hierarchically, using indentation to reveal the chronological flow of the conversations. You can find discussion groups dedicated to specific topics by using discussion group search engines, such as Google Groups, Yahoo Groups, Boardreader, and BoardTracker. Social networks also often have active discussion groups, but you need to join the social network to search for and join these groups.

FIGURE D-2: Home page of a LinkedIn member

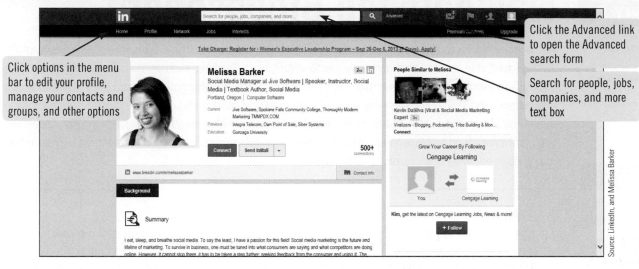

Click options in the menu bar to edit your profile, manage your contacts and groups, and other options

Click the Advanced link to open the Advanced search form

Search for people, jobs, companies, and more text box

FIGURE D-3: LinkedIn's Advanced People Search page

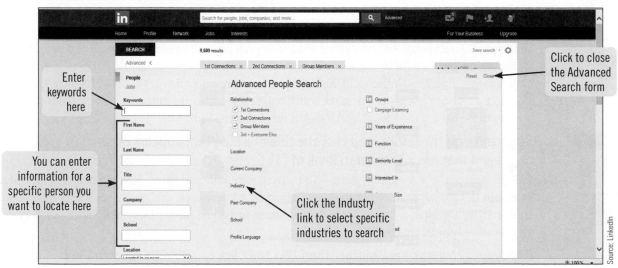

Enter keywords here

You can enter information for a specific person you want to locate here

Click the Industry link to select specific industries to search

Click to close the Advanced Search form

FIGURE D-4: Search results for wind energy experts in the Renewable & Environment industry

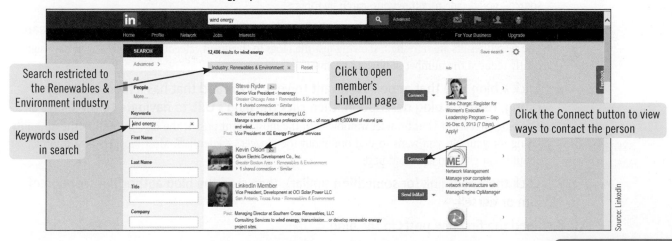

Search restricted to the Renewables & Environment industry

Keywords used in search

Click to open member's LinkedIn page

Click the Connect button to view ways to contact the person

Searching the Social Web

Navigate the Blogosphere

The **blogosphere** is made up of all blogs and their interconnections. The blogosphere continues to grow, in large part due to sites that allow people to create blogs for free, such as WordPress, which has over 140 million estimated unique monthly visitors. You can search for information on individual blog sites, but, fortunately, blog search engines have evolved to help people quickly and efficiently locate specific information in the blogosphere. **TABLE D-2** describes some of the popular blog search engines. **CASE** ▶ *To help you find more information and experts about biomass as a renewable energy, Bob suggests you search the blogosphere to find other informed opinions on this subject.*

STEPS

1. **Type technorati.com in your browser's Address bar, then press [Enter]**

   The Technorati home page appears. Note that the top of the page contains a variety of categories you can click to view popular blogs in each category. The page also includes a Search text box, and to the left of the Search text box are the Blogs and Posts buttons. These buttons allow you to specify whether you want the search to return blog titles or posts. Since you want to find experts in biomass as a renewable energy, you decide to search blogs in hopes of finding bloggers with this specialized knowledge.

2. **Click Blogs in the Search text box, type biomass renewable energy in the Search text box, then click the Search button**

   The search results appear, similar to those shown in **FIGURE D-5**. For each result, the blog title and the blog URL appears. A Technorati Authority rating and a Technorati Rank are given for each result as denoted in the "Auth:" column to the right of each result. Technorati Authority uses a proprietary algorithm to evaluate and rank a blog's standing and influence in the blogosphere on a scale from 0 to 1,000. You can see the Authority rating for a blog by clicking its link in the search results. The higher the Authority number the better. The number to the right of the "Auth" label indicates the Technorati Rank, with "1" being the highest.

QUICK TIP
You can click the page numbers at the top and bottom of the search results to see additional search returns.

3. **Scroll through the results, and click the title of a blog that appears relevant to your needs and that has a Technorati Rank of "1"**

   A description of the blog appears, along with its Technorati Authority rating. Scan the blog description to determine if it appears to belong to an expert in biomass as a renewable energy. You could click the URL to go directly to the blog. However, for now, you decide to explore further by refining your search using Technorati's advanced search features.

4. **Click your browser's Back button, then click the Click to refine this search link**

   The Refine search options form appears at the top of the page. Here you can choose to change whether blog titles or posts are returned. You can also choose whether to search in blogs, on news sites, or both (the "All" option). In addition, you can filter your search by topic and Authority rating. Finally, you can order search results by relevance (the default) or date. To narrow your search to experts dedicated to "green" energy sources, you decide to refine your search by topic.

5. **Click the Filter by list arrow next to "All topics", click Green, then click Refine this search**

   The search results are refreshed, showing just the blogs in the green category. Notice that you have significantly reduced the number of blogs to examine.

6. **Click a blog title that appears relevant to your needs and that has a high Authority rating, read the blog description, then click the blog's URL to navigate to the blog's site**

   The blog appears in your browser window with the most recent post at the top. To confirm the Authority rating for yourself, you want to find out about the blogger's credentials. Most bloggers post information about themselves on an About page.

7. **Click the About link (or something similar), then read the blog author's description of him or herself**

8. **Read the first few posts in the blog**

FIGURE D-5: Search results for *biomass renewable energy* on Technorati

TABLE D-2: Blog search engines

blog search engine	URL	search features
Google Blog Search	google.com/blogsearch	• Sort results by blog home page or post • Search results by how recently posted • Sort results by relevance or date
Technorati	technorati.com	• Search for posts or blog titles • Browse the blog directory • Search by tags • Filter results by Authority rating • Sort results by relevance or date
BlogSearchEngine	blogsearchengine.com	• Search by Categories (i.e., environmental or business) • Search for new blogs ("Freshest Finds")
Meltwater Icerocket	icerocket.com	• Search by exact phrase for posts • Restrict search to specific domains • Restrict search to a specific author and date range

Understanding RSS

RSS (Real Simple Syndication) is a protocol that gives you the ability to selectively subscribe to automatic updates from a wide variety of social media platforms. The updated content is often called a feed or channel. Most social media sites offer an RSS feed to their sites, as denoted by the 🔊 icon. An **RSS reader** lets you receive and view RSS feeds, typically showing the titles and brief descriptions of fresh content, making it simple to skim the list and then find and click a relevant item, displaying the entire article, post, or video. It is unlikely that the current vibrant and growing social web would exist without RSS. Without RSS (or a similar service), it would be necessary to manually visit each of these sites to discover and read new content, thus vastly restricting the scope and magnitude of the social web. Popular RSS readers include RSSOwl, Sage RSS Reader, as well as built-in RSS readers in products like Microsoft Internet Explorer and Outlook.

Scan Microblogs

Although there are other microblog sites, such as FriendFeed, Tumblr, and Plurk, Twitter's huge following and rich search capabilities make it the microblog of choice for research. There are more than 340 million tweets a day on Twitter. Twitter authors, or twitterers, make liberal use of tags to make it easier to locate a tweet about a particular topic. In addition, a tweet author can tag a tweet by using **hashtags**, which are words in a tweet that the author identifies by typing the pound, or hash, sign operator (#) before the word to create topical categories that others can search for. You can find tweets tagged with a specific hashtag by placing the hash sign operator in front of a word in the Search text box. Another powerful Twitter operator is the "at" sign (@). To use this operator, type the @ symbol in front a twitterer's name to return all messages that contain that name (e.g., @Melissa_Barker). And you can use the near: operator to find search terms tweeted by people near a specific location. **CASE** ▶ *At the renewable energy conference in Washington, D.C., you attended a panel discussion about geothermal energy. You decide to search for discussions about this topic using Twitter.*

STEPS

1. **Type twitter.com in your browser's Address bar, then press [Enter]**
   The Twitter home page appears. See **FIGURE D-6**.

2. **If you have a Twitter account and you are not already signed in, enter your username and password to sign in; if you do not have a Twitter account, enter your full name, email address, and a password, click Sign up for Twitter, then follow the instructions to create your profile page**
   FIGURE D-7 shows an example of a Twitter author's home page.

3. **Click in the Search text box, type geothermal energy, then click the Search button**
   A list of the most relevant tweets appears in chronological order. Each result begins with the name of the Twitter user, followed by the @ symbol with the Twitter user's abbreviated name and when the tweet was posted. The actual tweet appears below each listing, with a series of options, which vary depending upon the situation (e.g., Expand, View summary, View conversation, Reply, Retweet, Favorite, and More). In each message text, the key words from your search are in bold.

4. **To find the most recent tweets, click the All link at the top of the list**
   A new search results page appears listing the most recent tweets matching your search term, instead of the most relevant ones. You decide to use the hashtag search operator to search for tweets tagged with the hashtag *geothermal*.

5. **Delete the text in the Search text box, type #geothermal, then click the Search button**
   This search returns a list of all the tweets with the hashtag *geothermal*. Because tweeters do not use hashtag operators consistently, it may require a trial-and-error approach to find a hashtag that returns the results you want. You have heard that the twitterer whose user name is deepgreendesign posts interesting tweets, so you decide to use the @ search operator to find tweets that mention this user name.

6. **Replace the text in the Search text box with @deepgreendesign, then click the Search button**
   A list of all the messages that mention that user's name appears. When you search for tweets that mention a user name, you might see results that contain tweets that resemble a conversation; for example, a tweet posted in reply to a tweet by deepgreendesign might say "Thanks for that info."

FIGURE D-6: Twitter home page

Sign in here if you already have a Twitter account

Fill out this form to sign up for Twitter

FIGURE D-7: Author's page on Twitter

Enter a search phrase here

Search button

Post containing a hashtag

Post directed to this user

Search Video and Photo Sharing Sites

Learning Outcomes
• Locate videos on a video sharing site
• Find photos on a photo sharing site

A video sharing site, such as YouTube, lets users upload videos for public viewing. Typically, registered users are allowed to comment on videos and tag them with descriptive keywords to group them by topic, making it easier to locate similar videos. Photo sharing sites, such as Flickr, work much the same way. Many sites let users rank videos or photos, with the most popular images featured on the sites' home pages. Since videos and graphics are not text based, they are inherently hard to search using keywords. Fortunately, video and photo sharing sites (along with other third parties) have developed sophisticated search engines to facilitate this process. **CASE** *You heard at the conference that several cities in the Northwest are exploring the use of hydropower. You know little about this form of renewable energy, so Bob suggests you begin by finding an instructional video on the subject. You also need a photo to use in a newsletter you plan to send.*

STEPS

1. **Type youtube.com in your browser's Address bar, then press [Enter]**
   The YouTube home page appears with the Search text box at the top.

QUICK TIP
You can narrow video search returns to just the clips that have your keywords in their titles with the intitle: operator (for example, *intitle:hydroelectric*).

2. **Click in the Search text box, type how hydropower works, then click the Search button**
   A list of results appears. Identifying information about each video appears to the right of each thumbnail of a frame from each video, as shown in **FIGURE D-8**, including a link to the creator's YouTube **channel**, which is the home page of the account holder listing all the video clips uploaded by this person.

3. **Scroll through the results, then click the thumbnail or the title of one you want to view**
   When the video begins playing, thumbnails of related videos appear on the right; upon completion of the video, other related videos are displayed in the Play window. When you conduct a search on YouTube, the results are sorted by relevance, but you can change it so they are sorted by upload date, view count, or rating.

4. **Click the Back button in your browser, click Filters at the top of your search results to open a menu, then click View count beneath the Sort by heading**
   The results are sorted from the most watched to the least. The Filters button also provides options for narrowing results by the upload date, result type, duration, and features. Next, you need a photo for a newsletter.

5. **Type flickr.com in your browser's Address bar, then press [Enter]**
   The home page for Flickr appears, with a Search text box at the top.

QUICK TIP
Alternative ways to search Flickr are TagGalaxy, Compfight, and Flickriver.

6. **Click in the Search text box, type hydroelectric generator, then click the Search button**
   A list of image search results appears. To further refine your search, you decide to use the advanced search features in Flickr.

7. **Click the Advanced Search link below the Search text box**
   The Advanced Search form appears, as shown in **FIGURE D-9**. By default, the option of searching the full text of the photo descriptions is selected, as is the Photos / Videos check box in the Search by content type section, and the Photos & Videos option in the Search by media type section.

QUICK TIP
You can right-click a picture to select different sizes to display.

8. **Click the Screenshots / Screencasts and Illustration/Art / Animation/CGI check boxes in the Search by content type section, scroll to the bottom of the page, then click SEARCH**
   A list of image search results appears. You can click a result to display a larger version of the photo along with details on the creator of the image and how the image was created. If you click the name, that photographer's or organization's **photostream**—the Flickr home page of the account holder—appears.

FIGURE D-8: Search results for *how hydropower works* on YouTube

FIGURE D-9: Flickr Advanced Search page

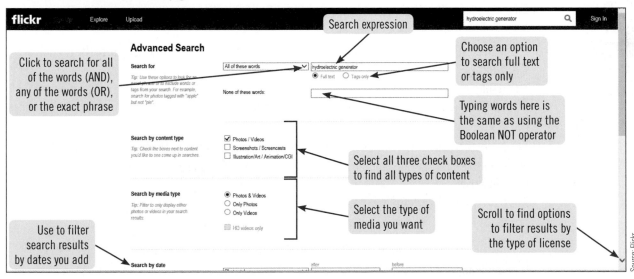

Understanding copyrights and licenses

Most of the images and clips on photo and video sharing sites are protected by copyright. Some images on Flickr.com are made available through a Creative Commons license, which allows content owners to describe the rights they retain while allowing them to share their content. There are several types of Creative Commons licenses, as described on their web site (creativecommons.org/licenses/) and on Flickr (flickr.com/creativecommons/). To check the copyright restrictions for a particular photo on Flickr, display the photo's page, and look for the license information under the "Additional info" heading. Photos that are not licensed under Creative Commons licenses will have "All rights reserved," "Request to license link," or something similar under the License heading. If you want to restrict your search to photos that have a Creative Commons license, on the Advanced Search page click the appropriate check box in the search form.

Search Social News Sites

Social news sites are good places to find links to popular news articles that other users liked. Some social news sites use human editors or a combination of votes and editors to select the stories that appear on their home pages. Highly frequented social news sites include Reddit, Digg, Slashdot, and Newsvine. You can find popular news stories and well-written, popular articles about specific topics quickly if you use the search engines on these sites. **CASE** ▶ *With Bob's urging, you decide to use social news sites to learn more about geothermal energy.*

STEPS

1. Type reddit.com in your browser's Address bar, then press [Enter]

The home page for Reddit appears. The most popular news stories as voted by users are displayed on the home page.

2. Click in the search reddit text box, type geothermal energy, then press [Enter]

The search results appear, similar to those shown in **FIGURE D-10**. The results are sorted by relevance. You can change the sort order or filter the results based upon when the articles were published. In addition, you can narrow results by selecting a "subreddit" category.

3. Click the /r/energy link in the too many results? section listing subreddit categories

The results for the geothermal energy articles found in the energy subreddit category appear. You want to find recent articles, so you decide to restrict the search results to those published during the last year. To do this, you'll use the "links from" options to filter the results. You can filter the results by this hour, this month, and this year.

4. Click the links from: all time link at the top of the search results list, and then click this year

The results change to display only those articles on geothermal energy published in the energy subreddit category in the last year. Impressed with articles you found using this social news site, you decide to try another.

5. Type slashdot.org in your browser's Address bar, then press [Enter]

The home page for Slashdot appears. The most popular stories, submissions, and blog posts are displayed on the home page.

6. Click in the Search text box, type geothermal energy, then press [Enter]

The search results appear, grouped by relevance and chronology, with the most recent articles at the top.

7. Scroll through the search results, then click the title of a relevant item

A synopsis appears below the item, as shown in **FIGURE D-11**, written by the person posting the article, or by a reader of the article. Most of these synopses contain links to relevant articles about the subject.

FIGURE D-10: Search results for *geothermal energy* on Reddit

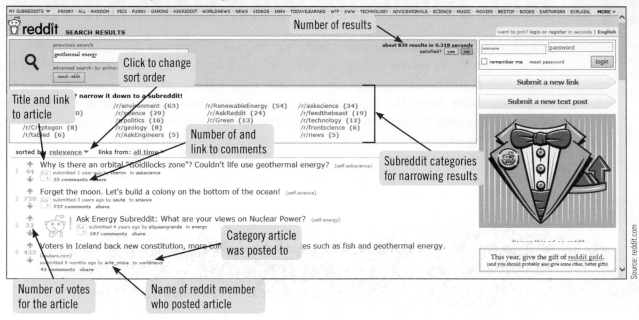

FIGURE D-11: Article summary on Slashdot.org

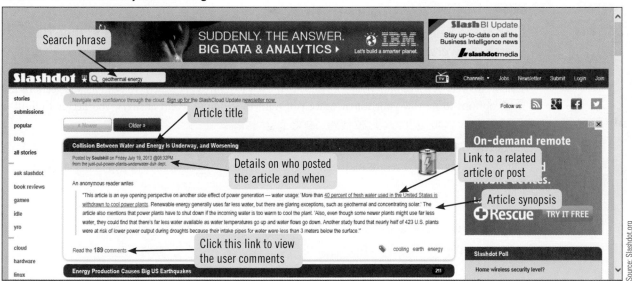

Social bookmarking sites

A social bookmarking site, such as Delicious or BlinkList, lets people store and describe their favorite web pages with tags, therefore allowing other users to search for popular content. Sometimes tags are presented as a **tag cloud**, or a word cloud, in which the font size of the text indicates how often the tag is used. Clicking a tag opens a page of results listing items associated with that tag. Social bookmarking and social news sites share many common characteristics; indeed, they are often cross-classified in both social media platform categories. However, people who use social bookmarking sites include links to web pages other than pages including news articles. These cross-disciplinary platforms have spawned niche-based news aggregators that focus on particular topics, such as Marketing Land (social media marketing) and Techmeme (technology news).

Find Answers with Q&A Sites

At a Q&A site, users can post a question using ordinary phrasing for others to answer. Most Q&A sites deliver fast answers by looking up questions that have already been asked. If you're lucky, the answer has already been posted in responses to an earlier question; otherwise, you will have to wait to see if someone answers your query. Some Q&A sites let you classify your question by category, increasing your odds it will be seen and answered by a person who knows about the subject. Popular Q&A sites include Answers.com, Yahoo! Answers, and Quora. Answers is unique in that it combines responses from common users with authoritative sources, such as WikiAnswers, ReferenceAnswers, and VideoAnswers, and international language Q&A communities. **CASE** *You are interested in learning more about biofuels. Bob, the reference librarian, suggests you use a Q&A site to inquire about them.*

STEPS

1. **Type answers.com in your browser's Address bar, then press [Enter]**
   The Answers home page appears, as shown in **FIGURE D-12**.

2. **Click in the Ask us anything text box, type What is biofuel?, then click Go**
   The search results for your question appear, similar to those shown in **FIGURE D-13**. You want to see the results from another Q&A site.

3. **Type answers.yahoo.com in your browser's Address bar, then press [Enter]**
   The Yahoo! Answers site appears. You need to have a Yahoo! account to ask a question of the Yahoo! community. If you don't have a Yahoo! account, you can use the Search text box next to the Search Answers button to search for existing questions and answers.

4. **Click in the Search text box at the top of the page, type What is ethanol? then click Search Answers**
   The search results display responses to various questions about ethanol fuel from community members of Yahoo! Answers. A list of options are provided to the left to refine your search. You can make selections from these options to narrow your search. Since you want to see more recent answers, you decide to limit the results to one year.

5. **Click the Date Submitted list box, click Last 1 year, then click Apply**
   Yahoo! Answers displays results for the questions about *ethanol fuel* that were posted in the last year.

FIGURE D-12: Answers home page

Type your search terms here →

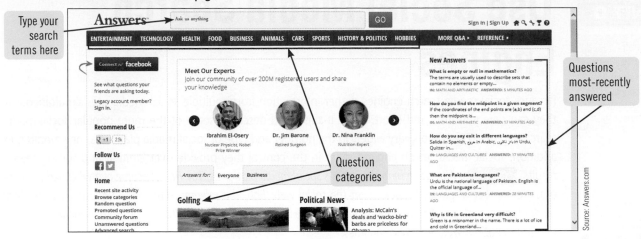

Question categories

Questions most-recently answered

Source: Answers.com

FIGURE D-13: Search results for *What is biofuel?* on Answers

Indicates where your answer came from

Answer to your question

Information on related subjects

Sponsored result

Use these buttons to fine tune your results

Source: Answers.com

Understanding a Wiki

Wikis, like a Q&A site, draw on the power of the masses to provide information. The largest, most popular one is Wikipedia. In addition, there are wiki sites, such as Wikia, which let people collaboratively build their own wikis, as well as wiki server software packages. Enterprises and academics were earlier adopters of wikis. A number of well-known corporations have used wikis internally for collaborative project management and information sharing. A few corporations have ventured into attempting collaboratively built customer support systems, without much success. Academic wikis include nLab for math, physics, and philosophy, and academicjobs.wikia.com for employment.

Use Social Media Search Engines

Learning
Outcome
• Search multiple
  social media
  search engines
  simultaneously

Because social media search engines gather information from multiple social media sites simultaneously, they can save you time and effort. **TABLE D-3** lists and describes some of the more popular social media search engines. These tools vary widely in the number and type of social media platforms they monitor. In addition, social media search engines differ in the control they provide over limiting and sorting search results. **CASE** *After searching the various social media platforms, you have become overwhelmed with the massive number of places to look at on the social web. Bob, the reference librarian, suggests using a social media search engine to find information on multiple social media sites simultaneously. You decide to search for information about wind energy companies.*

STEPS

1. **Type socialmention.com in your browser's Address bar, then press [Enter]**

   The Social Mention home page appears. See **FIGURE D-14**. It includes a search text box, and a list box from which you can choose which type of social media you want to search. The default is set to All.

2. **Click in the Search text box, type wind energy company, make sure All appears in the in list box, then click Search**

   After a few moments, a page with search results appears, as shown in **FIGURE D-15**. The search results show the page title, along with the source of the page. Note that the top of the page contains a variety of categories you can click to narrow your search (the default is All). In addition, you can use the Sort by and Results list boxes located above the search results to reorder the results based on Date or Source and how recently the item was posted.

3. **Scroll through the search results and click a link that appears relevant to your needs**

   A new window or tab opens, displaying the content. Take a moment to look it over. You decide to see what video clips are available to view about wind energy companies.

4. **Switch back to your Social Mention search results page**

   At the top of the panel to the left of the search results you see a variety of useful statistics, such as the time and frequency of mentions, and unique authors of the content. In addition, this panel includes a set of useful filters, such as Sentiment (i.e., how many of mentions have a positive, neutral, or negative tone), as well as Top Keywords, Top Users, Top Hashtags, and Sources. You can use these filters to refine the search results.

   TROUBLE
   If youtube is not
   listed under the
   Sources heading,
   select another source
   option.

5. **Scroll down and click the youtube link under the Sources heading in the left panel**

   After a few moments, your search results change to display only those from YouTube, displayed as a list of embedded videos. You can watch any video by clicking the play icon in the video play window.

6. **To remove the filters, click the Clear all filters link at the bottom of the left panel on the results page**

   Social Mention runs your original search query again, and after a moment, the search results page appears.

FIGURE D-14: Social Mention home page

Search text box

Set to search All social media sources

FIGURE D-15: Search results for *wind energy company* on Social Mention

Title, source, and when the page was found

Social media sources by which you can narrow your search

All social media sources searched

Number of mentions found

Statistics on your topic's appearance in social media

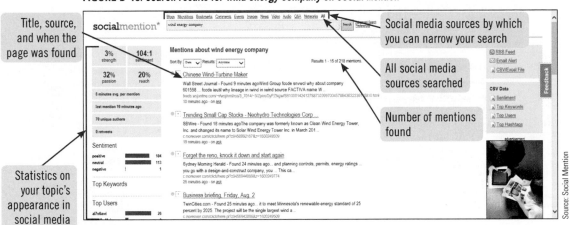

TABLE D-3: Social media search engines

social monitoring engines	URL	tool features
Social Mention	socialmention.com	• Search a wide variety of social media sites • Specify which social media categories
Addict-o-matic	addictomatic.com	• Search a wide variety of social media sites • Creates page with search results categorized by sources
Topsy	topsy.com	• Use Boolean commands • Restrict search to a date range
Whos Talkin	whostalkin.com	• Search over 60 social media sites • Provides a gadget to use from Google
48ers	48ers.com	• Searches Twitter, Facebook, Google Buzz, Digg, and Delicious • Provides links to current trends on social media sites

©2014 Cengage Learning

Understanding social media dashboards

A social media dashboard combines content from multiple social media platforms into a side-by-side format for easy viewing and access. Popular social media dashboards include Hootsuite, TweetDeck, Sprout Social, and NetVibes. Some of these dashboards provide social web demographics, scheduling of content publication, and sophisticated social media analytics. The cost of using these tools to monitor and participate in the social web ranges from free to sizable fees. However, social media dashboards can save you a great deal of time and effort, especially if you spend extended periods searching social media sites and contributing to them.

Practice

Concepts Review

Match each component of the Social Mention search results page shown in FIGURE D-16 **to an item in the list.**

FIGURE D-16

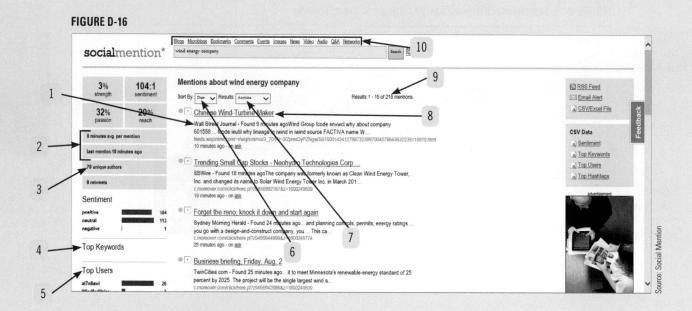

a. Statistics on time and frequency of mentions

b. Sort By Date

c. Source of article

d. Total number of results (mentions)

e. Top Keywords

f. Article title

g. Specifies search results can be from any time period

h. Top Users

i. Social media categories

j. Number of unique authors contributing content

Match each term with the statement that best describes it.

11. **Searching the social web**
12. **Microblog**
13. **Social media search engine**
14. **Blog**
15. **Social news site**
16. **Photo sharing site**
17. **Social network**

a. Enables people to easily establish relationships and virtual communities by sharing personal profiles, participating in groups, and exchanging private and public messages

b. Allows users to upload images for public or private sharing

c. A form of blogging, with the main difference being significant limits on the length of posts

d. A tool that lets you find information, usually in real time, from multiple social media sites simultaneously

e. Enables you to locate information using social media platforms

f. Allows users to submit links to news stories or other web pages by topic, and vote and comment on them

g. Enables users to post entries, such as commentaries and other material, including graphics or video

Select the best answer from the list of choices.

18. **Which of the following is not a social media platform?**
    a. Social networks
    b. TV news
    c. Blogs
    d. Q&A sites

19. **The most visited social media site is _____.**
    a. Facebook
    b. MySpace
    c. Twitter
    d. YouTube

20. **LinkedIn is a favorite social network for _____.**
    a. rock bands
    b. video enthusiasts
    c. photographers
    d. businesses

21. **You can use blog search engines to quickly search _____.**
    a. discussion groups
    b. Twitter
    c. the blogosphere
    d. all social networks

22. **Twitter users group topics together using _____.**
    a. hashtags
    b. search operators
    c. tweets
    d. @search

23. **To find an individual's collection of video clips on YouTube, you would check the person's YouTube _____ .**
    a. email address.
    b. blog
    c. tags
    d. channel

24. **Reddit is an example of a _____ .**
    a. photo sharing site
    b. video sharing site
    c. book sharing site
    d. social news site

25. **Social media search engines find information on multiple social media sites _____ .**
    a. sequentially
    b. in succession
    c. serially
    d. simultaneously

Skills Review

1. **Understand social media platforms.**
    a. Describe social networks.
    b. Explain how blogs work.
    c. Describe the main differences between blogs and microblogs.
    d. Describe what video and photo sharing sites do.
    e. Explain the function of social news sites.
    f. Describe how Q&A sites work.

2. **Search social networks.**
    a. Go to **linkedin.com**, then log into your profile.
    b. Use the LinkedIn Advanced People Search page to find employees that currently work in the Research industry with expertise in **renewable energy**. If requested by your instructor, print or save this page of results.
    c. Explore the search results to find a person with expertise in renewable energy.

3. **Navigate the blogosphere.**
    a. Go to **technorati.com**.
    b. Use Technorati's search tools to locate blogs about **geothermal energy**. If requested by your instructor, print or save this page of results.
    c. Examine the results, go to a blog with an authority rating over 300, if possible, and then examine several posts at the blog to judge the expertise of the owner.
    d. Return to your Technorati search results, and then refine the search to filter the results to those that fit in the Technology category. If requested by your instructor, print or save this page of results.
    e. Find another blog whose owner likely has expertise in geothermal energy and examine it.

Skills Review (continued)

4. **Scan microblogs.**

   a. Go to **twitter.com**.

   b. Search for tweets about **biomass energy**. If requested by your instructor, print or save this page of results.

   c. Examine the search results for messages with worthwhile information.

   d. Search for tweets tagged with the hashtag **#biomass**. If requested by your instructor, print or save this page of results.

   e. Search for tweets that mention the biomass company **wood2energy**, a company that posts tweets. If requested by your instructor, print or save this page of results.

5. **Search video and photo sharing sites.**

   a. Go to **youtube.com**.

   b. Search for a video that explains **how solar energy works**. If requested by your instructor, print or save this page of results.

   c. Sort the results by View count. If requested by your instructor, print or save this page of results.

   d. Watch the video that has been viewed the most often.

   e. Go to **flickr.com** and search for images on **wind farms**.

   f. Use Flickr's Advanced Search page to search for any type of graphic featuring **solar energy**. If requested by your instructor, print or save this page of results.

   g. Display the photographer's photostream. If requested by your instructor, print or save this page of results.

6. **Search social news sites.**

   a. Go to **reddit.com**.

   b. Search for news articles about **hydroelectric energy**.

   c. Filter the search results using the subreddit category of energy. If requested by your instructor, print or save this page of results.

   d. Go to **slashdot.org**.

   e. Search for recent news articles about **hydroelectric energy**. If requested by your instructor, print or save this page of results.

   f. Read some of the descriptions of the articles that look interesting.

7. **Find answers with Q&A sites.**

   a. Go to **answers.com**.

   b. Formulate and enter a search question to learn what **ocean thermal energy** is. If requested by your instructor, print or save this page of results.

   c. Examine the sources and quality of the information returned by Answers.com.

   d. Go to **answers.yahoo.com**.

   e. Search for answers about **biomass energy**.

   f. Refine the search to return results that were published in the Last 90 days. If requested by your instructor, print or save this page of results.

Skills Review (continued)

8. Use social media search engines.

  a. Go to **socialmention.com**.

  b. Search for a **solar energy company** in all social media categories. If requested by your instructor, print or save this page of results.

  c. Explore a few of the search results to locate companies that specialize in solar energy.

  d. Filter the results to display only those results from **delicious**, the social bookmarking site. If requested by your instructor, print or save this page of results.

  e. Remove all filters and run the search again.

Independent Challenge 1

Job interviews have become highly competitive, with tougher questions, better-trained interviewers, and well-prepared applicants. Your chances of performing well in a job interview can be improved with practice and insightful tips. Use social media to find a job training video, with advice on how to practice for a job interview.

  a. Go to **youtube.com**.

  b. Conduct a search using the query **how practice "job interview"**. If requested by your instructor, print or save this page of results.

  c. Scroll down the list of videos on the results page, and then watch one that looks useful.

  d. Conduct another search for **video resume tips**. If requested by your instructor, print or save this page of results.

  e. Scroll down the list of videos, and then watch one that provides tips on creating a video resume.

  f. Go to **technorati.com** and search for posts in the business category for ideas on preparing for a job interview. If requested by your instructor, print or save this page of results.

  g. Which social media platform did you find most helpful in finding tips and strategies for preparing for a job interview?

Independent Challenge 2

You work in advertising, and your company is considering expanding to social media marketing. You have heard about this topic and want to learn more.

  a. Go to **icerocket.com**.

  b. If necessary, click the BLOGS tab, and then use the Search text box to conduct a search of the blogs about **social media marketing**. If requested by your instructor, print or save this page of results.

  c. Explore several of the top blogs about the topic, and read a few relevant posts.

  d. Return to **icerocket.com**, click the SEARCH ALL tab at the top of the home page to use the social media search engine, and then search again for information about **social media marketing**. If requested by your instructor, print or save this page of results.

  e. Scroll the results page, and notice the results are organized by different social media platforms. Explore a few of the results listed under the Twitter heading, and then click one to go to the author's Twitter home page. If requested by your instructor, print or save this page.

Independent Challenge 3

You want to take a vacation, but you have never been outside the country. You want to see what people are saying about traveling abroad.

a. Go to **twitter.com**.

b. Conduct a search using the query **travelling abroad**. If requested by your instructor, print or save this page of results.

c. Scroll down the list of results, and then click one that seems to have general information about travelling abroad.

d. Read the information, and then return to your Twitter search results.

e. Conduct a search using the query **travel tips** with a hashtag in front of each term. If requested by your instructor, print or save this page of results.

f. Scroll down the list of results, and then read several of the tips.

g. Go to **reddit.com** and search for tips about travelling to Mexico. Refine your search to the **/r/travel** subreddit category. If requested by your instructor, print or save this page of results.

h. Go to **answers.com** and find out the **population of Mexico**. If requested by your instructor, print or save this page of results.

Independent Challenge 4: Explore

You have heard Google is a great place to work. You want to check out some of the people that work there using a social network.

a. Go to **linkedin.com**, and then log into your profile.

b. Find people who currently work at Google. If requested by your instructor, print or save this page of results.

c. Explore several of the Google employee pages, paying special attention to their qualifications.

d. Filter the search to include only those people that include the keyword **manager**. If requested by your instructor, print or save this page of results.

e. Click the Jobs link in the LinkedIn menu bar at the top of the page, use the Search box in the Search for jobs section to search for **software engineer** positions.

f. Use the Advanced Jobs Search form to look for positions with the job title **software engineer** at the company **Google**, and then explore the results.

g. Narrow the results to within 50 miles of your zip code, and then explore the results. (If no results were returned from the previous search at Google, first remove *Google* from the Company text box.) If requested by your instructor, print or save this page of results.

h. If you have a Facebook account, go to **facebook.com**, then search Facebook to find Google's Facebook page. If requested by your instructor, print or save this page of results.

i. If you do not have a Facebook account, go to **google.com**, type **google site:facebook.com** in the Search text box to use the site operator to search for the text *Google* on Facebook. If requested by your instructor, print or save this page of results. Click the link to Google's Facebook page, which is probably the first result in the list of results.

j. Examine the page, and pay attention to the other Google pages listed under "Likes." Consider visiting these pages to find out more about the company.

Visual Workshop

Use Flickr.com to find the photograph shown in **FIGURE D-17**. This photograph shows the Frederiksborg Castle in Copenhagen, Denmark. If requested by your instructor, print or save the page on the photo sharing site on which this photo is displayed.

FIGURE D-17

Source: Library of Congress

Glossary

Algorithm A mathematical formula used by a search engine to rank each web site returned in search results according to the terms used in the search query.

AND A Boolean operator that when used to connect keywords in a search query requires that each keyword connected by it must be on a web page for that web page to be included in the results.

Annotation In a subject guide, a summary or review of a web page, usually written by experts, such as professionals, academics in the field, or librarians.

Blog A web site on which people post commentaries and invite comments from viewers.

Blogosphere All blog content and the interconnections that form a social network.

Boolean algebra *See* Boolean logic.

Boolean logic The field of mathematics that defines how Boolean operators manipulate large sets of data by connecting keywords with Boolean operators. *Also called* Boolean algebra.

Boolean operators Command words such as AND, OR, and AND NOT that narrow, expand, or restrict a search based on Boolean logic.

Cached page A copy of a web page that resides on a search engine's computer.

Channel The home page of a YouTube account holder.

Citation format A style guide that standardizes references to resources like books, magazine articles, and web pages; common formats are those by MLA (Modern Language Association) and APA (American Psychological Association).

Complex search query A search query that uses Boolean operators to define the relationships between keywords and phrases in a way that search tools can interpret.

Deep web The part of the web inaccessible to search engine spiders and consisting primarily of information housed in databases. *Also called* invisible web.

Default operator The Boolean operator that a search engine automatically uses in a query, whether typed as part of the query or not. Most search engines default to the AND operator, although a few default to the OR operator.

Discussion group A way for people to conduct conversations online by exchanging messages asynchronously.

Discussion forum *See* discussion group.

Distributed subject guide A subject guide created by a variety of editors working somewhat independently and usually stored on numerous computers located around the country or the world.

Drill down To click through subject headings (or topics or categories) to reach relevant links.

Dynamically generated web page A web page generated by a database in response to a specific query.

Evaluative criteria Standards used to determine if a web site is appropriate for your needs, including considerations of organization, authority, objectivity, accuracy, scope, and currency.

Hashtag A word in a tweet that the author identifies by typing the pound, or hash, sign operator (#) before the word to create topical categories that others can search for.

Hierarchy A ranked order.

Internet A vast global network of interconnected networks.

Internet directory *See* Subject guide.

Internet search tool A service that helps locate information on the web, including search engines, metasearch engines, subject guides, specialized search engines, and social media search engines.

Intersection The place where two sets overlap in a Venn diagram.

Invisible web *See* deep web.

Keyword An important word that describes a major concept of your search topic.

Keyword generator A tool that produces related keywords by using synonyms, plurals, misspellings, and other grammatical inflections.

Metasearch engine A search tool that searches the indexes of multiple search engines simultaneously.

Microblog A blog that significantly limits the length of posts.

Mnemonic Assisting or aiding memory.

Not A Boolean operator that when used to connect keywords in a search query requires that each keyword connected by it must *not* be on a web page for that web page to be included in the results.

News aggregator A web site that collects headlines from news sources and lists them as links.

Online reference source A digital version of an almanac, dictionary, encyclopedia, and other similar resources available on the Internet.

OR A Boolean operator that when used to connect keywords in a search query requires that at least one of the keywords connected by it appears on a web page for that web page to be included in the results.

Periodical database A specialized database that usually requires a paid subscription, is available only at libraries, and contains the full text of articles from periodicals, such as newspapers, magazines, and journals.

Photo sharing site A web site on which people upload and share photos.

Photostream The home page of the account holder on Flickr.

Phrase search To force a search tool to search only for pages containing two or more words together in a certain order; typically, quotation marks are used around the words to indicate that they should be searched as a phrase.

Portal A large web gateway providing access to huge amounts of information via search engines, news, shopping, email, chat, and more. *See also* vortal.

Post (n.) A published blog entry.

Post (v.) To publish a blog entry or comment.

Q&A site *See* question-and-answer site.

Query *See* search query.

Question-and-answer (Q&A) site A social search tool that lets you pose a question and receive answers from anyone willing to reply.

RSS (Really Simple Syndication) A protocol that gives you the ability to selectively subscribe to automatic updates from a wide variety of social media platforms.

RSS reader Software that allows you to receive and view RSS feeds.

Search engine A search tool, usually indexed by spiders, that locates web pages containing the keywords entered in a search form.

Search engine optimization (SEO) The process of fine-tuning a web site so that it ranks at the top of search engine results.

Search query Keywords, phrases, and Boolean operators entered into a search form that the search tool uses to search its index.

Search result A web page returned by a search tool in response to a search.

Set A collection of objects; in a Venn diagram, sets are represented by circles.

Social bookmarking site A site on which people store and describe their favorite web pages with descriptors (tags), allowing you to search for popular content.

Social media platform How social media is presented on the web, including social networks, blogs, microblogs, video and photo sharing sites, social news sites, Q&A sites, bookmarking sites, news aggregators, and wiki sites.

Social media search engine A search tool that searches only the social web.

Social media site A web site that contains content from a type of social media platform.

Social network An online community where people form relationships based on everything from friendship and workplace affiliations to common interests and shared beliefs.

Social news site A web site that allows users to submit news stories or other web pages and vote on news stories posted by others.

Social web The collection of social media sites on the web.

Specialized search engine A search engine that limits the web pages it indexes by subject.

Spider A computer program that scans, or crawls, the web to index web pages without making judgments regarding the value of indexing a page, as human indexers do.

Stop word A common word, such as *a, and, the, for,* or *of,* that is not normally searched by search tools.

Subject directory *See* Subject guide.

Subject guide A search tool that hierarchically arranges links to web pages. The links are evaluated and annotated by people, usually subject specialists or librarians, rather than spiders. *Also called* Internet directory, subject directory, or subject tree.

Subject tree *See* Subject guide.

Surface web *See* visible web.

Synonym A word that has a similar meaning to another word.

Syntax The rules of a language, like grammar, that standardize usage.

Tag A key word that identifies the contents of blog and microblog posts, videos, photos, articles, and questions on Q&A sites to give search engines another keyword to index.

Tag cloud A presentation of tags in which the font size of the text indicates how often the tag is used.

Thread A subtopic in a discussion group, arranged in chronological order.

Trending search A current, popular search phrase on the Internet.

Union The combination of two sets in a Venn diagram.

Venn diagram A drawing, typically comprised of intersecting circles, used to illustrate Boolean logic or searches using Boolean operators.

Video sharing site A web site on which people upload and share videos.

Visible web The portion of the web that is indexed by search engine spiders; also can refer to parts of the web that, although not crawled by spiders, are indexed by subject guides. *Also called* surface web.

Vortal Short for vertical portal, a portal that focuses on only one topic or industry.

Web log *See* blog.

wiki Server software that lets anyone create and modify web page content.

World Wide Web An enormous repository of information stored on millions of computers all over the world.

Index